study companion

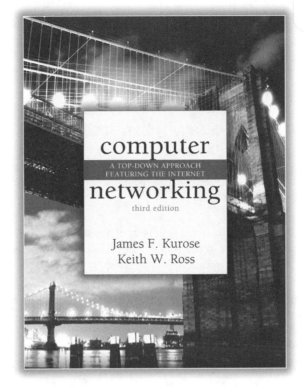

computer

A TOP-DOWN APPROACH
FEATURING THE INTERNET

networking

third edition

James F. Kurose
Keith W. Ross

James F. Kurose

University of Massachusetts, Amherst

Keith W. Ross

Polytechnic University

PEARSON

Addison
Wesley

Boston San Francisco New York
London Toronto Sydney Tokyo Singapore Madrid
Mexico City Munich Paris Cape Town Hong Kong Montreal

Publisher	Greg Tobin
Executive Editor	Michael Hirsch
Editorial Assistant	Lindsey Triebel
Senior Production Supervisor	Marilyn Lloyd
Marketing Manager	Michelle Brown
Marketing Assistant	Dana Lopreato
Senior Manufacturing Buyer	Carol Melville
Cover Image	© 2004 Photodisc
Composition and Illustrations	Laura Wiegleb

Access the latest information about Addison-Wesley titles from our World Wide Web site:
http://www.aw-bc.com/computing

Many of the designations used by manufacturers and sellers to distinguish their products are claimed as trademarks. Where those designations appear in this book, and Addison-Wesley was aware of a trademark claim, the designations have been printed in initial caps or all caps.

The programs and applications presented in this book have been included for their instructional value. They have been tested with care, but are not guaranteed for any particular purpose. The publisher does not offer any warranties or representations, nor does it accept any liabilities with respect to the programs or applications.

ISBN 0-321-41990-1

1 2 3 4 5 6 7 8 9 10—CRS—09 08 07 06

Preface

Why This Study Companion?

Since the first edition of *Computer Networking: A Top-Down Approach Featuring the Internet* (now in its third edition), we have received e-mail from hundreds of students from around the world. Sometimes students e-mail questions about content or comments (usually favorable!) about our book. But the most frequent e-mails we receive ask us for solutions to the end-of-chapter problems or for additional examples of material covered in the textbook. This *Study Companion* is our response.

This study companion not only provides additional examples, but also offers new material that will be valuable in helping students master the content in the textbook. We provide the following for each chapter:

♦ **A "top-ten" list of concepts covered in each chapter.** As we teach, often we explicitly tell students what we think are the two or three most important concepts that we've covered in class. Sometimes we ask our students what *they* think are the most important points covered. It's our way to emphasize and synthesize the key ideas among the many concepts covered in class. In this spirit, as a way to emphasize what *we* think are the most important ideas covered in each chapter of the textbook, we provide a top-ten list (with apologies to David Letterman) of important concepts for students to take away from each chapter. For a few chapters, there are so many important ideas, that the list extends a bit beyond 10; for a few other chapters, the list is a bit shorter. But, in spirit, they are all meant to be top-ten lists.

♦ **Solved problems, with commentary.** For each chapter, we provide questions and solutions that cover important material from the chapter. Often these problems are similar (but not identical!) to the end-of-chapter problems in the textbook—which is not surprising since the pedagogical goal of the end of chapter problems is to help students test and refine their understanding of the key material in the chapter. We list the problems first, followed by the solutions. We encourage readers to try to answer the questions (without peeking at the answers!) before studying the solutions.

We hope that you find the material in this study companion valuable. As always, we welcome comments, questions, and suggestions. We really enjoy hearing from our readers! In particular, if you have ideas that you think would be valuable material for future editions of this study companion, we hope you'll let us know.

Jim Kurose
kurose@cs.umass.edu
Keith Ross
ross@poly.edu

Contents

Computer Networks and the Internet

Most Important Ideas and Concepts from Chapter 1

- **Nuts and bolts of computer networks.** Computer networks consist of end systems, packet switches, and communication links. End systems—also called hosts—include desktop PCs, laptops, hand-held network devices (including cell phones, PDAs, and BlackBerries), sensors, and servers (such as Web and mail servers). Just as cities are interconnected by a network of roads and intersections, end systems of a computer network are interconnected by a network of communication links and packet switches. Communication links can be wired or wireless.

- **Distributed applications.** A computer network enables distributed applications. A distributed application runs on end systems and exchanges data via the computer network. Distributed applications include Web surfing, e-mail, instant messaging, Internet phone, distributed games, peer-to-peer file sharing, television distribution, and video conferencing. New distributed applications continue to be invented and deployed on the Internet.

- **Packet switching.** When one end system sends data to another end system, the sending end system breaks the data into chunks, called packets. Similar to the process of delivering post-office mail, the Internet transports each packet separately, routing a packet to its destination using a destination address that is written into the packet. When a packet switch receives a packet, it uses the packet's destination address to determine on which link it should forward the packet. Thus, a packet switch performs "packet switching," forwarding incoming packets to outgoing links packet by packet. Also, packet switches typically "store and forward" packets—that is, before a switch begins to forward a packet on an outgoing link, first it receives and stores the entire packet.

- **Protocol.** A protocol defines the format and order of messages exchanged between two or more communication entities, as well as the actions taken on the transmission and/or receipt of a message or other event. Computer networks make extensive use of protocols. Figure 1.2 (page 7 in your textbook) provides an analogy between a human protocol and a computer network protocol for messages exchanged between a Web browser and a Web server. In this example, first, the Web browser sends an introductory message to the server; next, the server responds with its own introductory message; then, the browser sends another message, requesting a specific Web page; and finally, the server sends a last message, which includes the requested Web page.

- **Circuit-switching.** Computer networks constitute one major class of communication networks. Another major class of communication networks is traditional digital telephone networks. Traditional digital telephone networks do not use packet switching to move data from a source to a destination; they use a technique known as circuit switching. In circuit switching, before transmitting data between two end systems, the network establishes a dedicated end-to-end connection between the end systems and reserves bandwidth in each link along the connection. The reserved connection bandwidth is "wasted" whenever the end systems are not sending data.

♦ **Physical media and access networks.** The communication links in a computer network may have different physical media types. Dial-up modem links, DSL, and most Ethernet links are made of copper wire. Cable links are made of coaxial cable. Long-haul Internet backbone links are made of fiber optics. In addition to these wired links, there is a plethora of wireless links, including Wi-Fi, Bluetooth®, and satellite. An access link is a link that connects the end system to the Internet. Access links can be copper wire, coaxial cable, fiber optics or wireless. A tremendous variety of media types can be found on the Internet.

♦ **Network of networks.** The Internet consists of many interconnected networks, each of which is called an Internet Service Provider (ISP). Each ISP is a network of packet switches and communication links. Thus, the Internet is a network of networks. ISPs are roughly organized in a hierarchy. ISPs at the bottom of the hierarchy access ISPs such as residential ISPs, university ISPs, and enterprise ISPs. ISPs at the top of the hierarchy are called tier-1 ISPs and typically include long-haul intra- and intercontinental fiber links. Tier-n ISPs provide service—for a price—to tier-(n+1) ISPs. Each ISP is independently managed. However, ISPs employ a common protocol suite called the Internet Protocol, which is better known as IP.

♦ **Transmission and propagation delays.** Transmission and propagation delays play a critical role in the performance of many distributed applications. Perhaps the best way to understand transmission and propagation delays and their differences is to work with the Transmission versus Propagation delay applet on the textbook's Web site. The propagation delay over a link is the time it takes a bit to travel from one end of the link to the other. It is equal to the length of the link divided by the propagation speed of the link's physical medium. The transmission delay is a quantity that relates to packets and not bits. The transmission delay for a link is equal to the number of bits in the packet divided by the transmission rate of the link. It is the amount of time it takes to push the packet onto the link. Once a bit is pushed onto a link it needs to propagate to the other end. The total delay across a link is equal to the sum of the transmission delay and the propagation delay.

♦ **Queuing delay and packet loss.** Many packets can arrive at a packet switch roughly at the same time. If these packets need to be forwarded on the same outbound link, all but one will have to "queue," that is, wait to be transmitted. This waiting introduces a queuing delay. Furthermore, if the queue of packets becomes very large, the packet switch's buffer may become exhausted, causing packets to be dropped or "lost." Queuing delay and packet loss can severely impact the performance of an application.

♦ **Protocol layers.** A typical computer network makes use of many protocols—easily hundreds. To deal with this complexity, the protocols are organized into layers. These protocol layers are arranged in a "stack." For example, the Internet organizes its protocols into five layers—namely, from top to bottom: application layer, transport layer, network layer, link layer, and physical layer. The protocols of layer n use the services provided by the protocols at the layer n − 1 (the layer below). This abstract concept, often difficult to grasp at first, will become clearer as we delve into the different protocol layers.

With the application-layer as the highest layer in the protocol stack, one can say that *all* other layers in the stack exist only to provide services to the application. Indeed this is the case, as applications are the *raison d'être* for computer networks. Without networked applications, there would be no need for computer networks in the first place!

♦ **Encapsulation.** When the sender-side application-layer process passes an application-level data unit (an application message) to the transport layer, that message becomes the *payload* of the transport-layer segment, which also contains additional transport-layer header information, for example, information that will allow the transport layer at the receiver side to deliver a message to the correct receiver-side application. Conceptually, one can think of the transport-layer segment as an envelope with some information on the outside of the envelope (the segment's header fields) and the application-layer payload as a message within the envelope. The transport layer passes the transport-layer segment to the network layer. The segment becomes the payload of the network-layer *datagram*, which has additional fields used by the network layer (for example, the address of the receiver). Conceptually, one can think of the transport-layer segment as an envelope within an envelope, with some information on the outside of the network-layer envelope. Finally, the network layer datagram is passed to the link layer, which encapsulates the datagram within a link-layer *frame*.

Continuing with our envelope analogy, a receiver-side protocol at layer n will look at the header information on the envelope. The protocol may pass the envelope back to the lower layer (for example, for forwarding to another node), or open the envelope and extract the upper-layer payload, and pass that upper-layer envelope up to layer n + 1. Like layering, the concept of encapsulation can be difficult to grasp at first. However, the technique is used so often throughout the textbook, that it will soon become second nature.

Review Questions

This section provides additional study questions. Answers to each question are provided in the next section.

1. **Packets in the Internet.** Suppose end system A wants to send a large file to end system B. On a very high level, describe how end system A creates packets from the file. When one of these packets arrives to a packet switch, what information in the packet does the switch use to determine the link onto which the packet is forwarded? Why is packet switching analogous to driving from one city to another and asking directions along the way?

2. **Protocol.** A protocol defines the format and order of messages exchanged between two or more communication entities, as well as the actions taken on the transmission and/or receipt of a message or other event. Describe the protocol for downloading a Web page, as shown in Figure 1.2 (page 7 in your textbook).

3. **Circuit switching.** What are the two most common multiplexing techniques used in circuit switching?

4. **Circuit switching versus packet switching.**

   a. Suppose that all of the network sources send data at a constant bit rate. Would packet-switching or circuit-switching be more desirable in this case? Why?

   b. Suppose that all of the network sources are bursty—that they only occasionally have data to send. Would packet-switching or circuit switching be more desirable in this case? Why?

5. **More on circuit switching.** Suppose users share a 1 Mbps link. Also suppose each user requires 500 kbps when transmitting, but each user transmits only 10 percent of the time. (See the discussion on Packet Switching Versus Circuit Switching in Section 1.1 in your textbook.)

   a. When circuit switching is used, how many users can be supported?

   b. For the remainder of this question, suppose packet switching is used. Why will there be essentially no queuing delay before the link if two or fewer users transmit simultaneously? Why will there be a queuing delay if three users transmit simultaneously?

   c. Find the probability that a given user is transmitting.

   d. Suppose there are three users. Find the probability that at any given time, all three users are transmitting simultaneously. Find the fraction of time during which the queue grows.

6. **Network of networks.** List four characteristics of a tier-1 ISP.

7. **More on network of networks.** Discuss the economic relationship among tier-1 ISPs. Discuss the economic relationship between tier-1 and tier-2 ISPs.

8. **Propagation delay.** How long does it take a packet of length 1,000 bytes to propagate over a link of distance 5,000 km, propagation speed 2.5×10^8 m/s, and transmission rate 1 Mbps? Generally, how long does it take a packet of length L to propagate over a link of distance d, propagation speed s, and transmission rate R bps? Does this delay depend on packet length? Does this delay depend on transmission rate?

9. **Transmission delay.** How long does it take to transmit a packet of length 1,000 bytes a link of distance 5,000 km, propagation speed 2.5×10^8 m/s, and transmission rate 1 Mbps? Generally, how long does it take to transmit a packet of length L over a link of distance d, propagation speed s, and transmission rate R bps? Does this delay depend on the length of the link? Does this delay depend on the propagation speed of the link?

10. **Transmission delay and propagation delay.** Consider two packet switches directly connected by a link of 5000 km, propagation speed 2.5×10^8 m/s, and transmission rate 1 Mbps. How long does it take to move a packet of length 1,000 bytes from one packet switch to the other packet switch? Generally, how long does it take to move a packet of length L over a link of distance d, propagation speed s, and transmission rate R bps?

11. **Delays with multiple links.** Consider a packet of length L which begins at end system A, travels over one link to a packet switch, and travels from the packet switch over a second link to a destination end system. Let d_i, s_i and R_i denote the length, propagation speed, and transmission rate of link i, for $i = 1, 2$. The packet switch delays each packet by d_{proc}. Assuming no queuing delays, in terms of d_i, s_i, R_i, $(i = 1, 2)$ and L, what is the total end-to-end delay for the packet? Suppose the packet is 1,000 bytes, the propagation speed on both links is 2.5×10^8 m/s, the transmission rates of both links is 1 Mbps, the packet switch processing delay is 1 msec, the length of the first link is 4,000 km, and the length of the last link is 1,000 km. For these values, what is the end-to-end delay?

12. **Store and forwarding.** In Question 11, suppose $R_1 = R_2 = R$ and $d_{proc} = 0$. Furthermore, suppose the packet switch does not store-and-forward packets but instead immediately transmits each bit it receives before waiting for the packet to arrive. What is the end-to-end delay?

13. **Queuing delay.** A packet switch receives a packet and determines the outbound link to which the packet should be forwarded. At packet arrival, one other packet is half transmitted on this outbound link and three other packets are waiting to be transmitted. Packets are transmitted in order of arrival. Suppose all packets are 1,000 bytes and the link rate is 1 Mbps. What is the queuing delay for the packet? Generally, what is the queuing delay when all packets

have length L, the transmission rate is R, x bits of the currently transmitted packet have been transmitted, and N packets are already in the queue?

14. **Average queuing delay.** Suppose N packets arrive simultaneously to a link at which no packets are currently being transmitted or queued. Each packet is of length L and the link has a transmission rate R. What is the average queuing delay for the N packets?

15. **Queuing delay with random arrivals.** Consider a link of rate R = 1 Mbps. Suppose packets of size L = 1,250 bytes arrive "randomly" to the link at a rate of 1 packet/sec. Let I = La/R denote the traffic intensity. Suppose the average queuing delays at the input to this link can be modeled as [I/(1 − I)] × [L/R] as long as I < 1. The average total delay is the queuing delay plus the transmission delay. Find the average queuing delay and average total delay for a = 30, 60, 90, and 99 packets/sec.

16. **Traceroute.** Consider the traceroute output on page 44 of the textbook:

```
1 cs-gw (128.119.240.254) 1.009 ms
2 128.119.3.154 (128.119.3.154) 0.931 ms
3 border4-rt-gi-1-3.gw.umass.edu (128.119.2.194) 1.032 ms
4 acr1-ge-2-1-0.Boston.cw.net (208.172.51.129) 10.006 ms
5 agr4-loopback.NewYork.cw.net (206.24.194.104) 12.272 ms
6 acr2-loopback.NewYork.cw.net (206.24.194.62) 13.225 ms
7 pos10-2.core2.NewYork1.Level3.net (209.244.160.133) 12.218 ms
8 gige9-1-52.hsipaccess1.NewYork1.Level3.net (64.159.17.39) 13.081 ms
9 p0-0.polyu.bbnplanet.net (4.25.109.122) 12.716 ms
10 cis.poly.edu (128.238.32.126) 14.080 ms
```

Here, we display only the first round-trip delay (rather than three delays) for each router. Explain why the delays sometimes decrease from one router to the next. Which link has the largest delay? Which link has the second largest delay? Where are these links located?

17. **Circuit switching.** Consider sending a packet of F bits over a path of Q links. Each link transmits at R bps. The network is lightly loaded so that there are no queuing delays. Propagation delay is also negligible.

   a. Suppose the network is a packet-switched datagram network and a connection-oriented service is used. Suppose each packet has h × F bits of header where 0 < h < 1. Assuming t_s setup time, how long does it take to send the packet?

   b. Suppose that the network is a circuit-switched network. Furthermore, suppose that the transmission rate of the circuit between source and destination is R/24 bps. Assuming t_s setup time and no bits of header appended to the packet, how long does it take to send the packet?

    c. When is the delay longer for packet switching than for circuit switching assuming h = 0.5? Interpret your result.

18. **Protocol layers.**

    a. What are the five protocol layers, from top to bottom, in the Internet?

    b. For each of the five layers, what is the name of the packets processed at the layer?

    c. An end-system processes up to which layer?

    d. A router processes up to which layer?

    e. A link-layer switch processes up to which layer?

Answers to Review Questions

1. End system A breaks the large file into chunks. To each chunk it adds a header, generating multiple packets from the file. The header in each packet includes the address of the destination: end system B. The packet switch uses the destination address to determine the outgoing link. Asking which road to take is analogous to a packet asking which outgoing link it should be forwarded on, given the packet's address. (The driving analogy is discussed on page 23 of your textbook.)

2. The protocol specifies that four messages are to be sent, in a specific order: first a TCP connection request message from client to server; then a TCP connection reply message from server to client; then an HTTP request for a specific Web object from client to server; and finally, a response message from server to client, including the requested object. The protocol also specifies the specific format of each of these messages. Note: This example is for illustrative purposes; it is not completely accurate, as we will see in Chapter 2.

3. Frequency division multiplexing, which partitions the bandwidth in a link using frequency bands, such as in FM radio; and time division multiplexing, which partitions time in a link with a revolving frame, giving each connection the same slot in the revolving frame.

4. a. Circuit-switching is more desirable here because there are no statistical multiplexing gains to be had, and by using circuits, each connection will get a constant amount of bandwidth that matches its CBR rate. On the other hand, circuit-switching has more overhead in terms of signaling needed to set up the call, so there is an argument that packet-switching is preferable here since there is no call setup overhead with packet-switching. If this were an exam question either answer would be correct (as long as you provide the correct reasoning!).

   b. Packet-switching is better here because there are statistical multiplexing gains—when a source does not have data to send, it will not be allocated bandwidth (it would be unused when the source had nothing to send). With packet-switching, this bandwidth is available for use by other sources.

5. a. Two users, each getting a dedicated 500 kbps.

   b. If two users transmit simultaneously, the input rate is a constant 1 Mbps. Since the link is also 1 Mbps, there will be no queuing delay. If three users transmit simultaneously, then the input rate is a constant 1.5 Mbps. Since the maximum output rate is 1 Mbps, bits will build up in a queue at a rate of 0.5 Mbps. After one second, the queue length will be approximately 500,000 bits.

   c. Since each user is transmitting 10 percent of the time, the probability that a user is transmitting at any instant is 0.1.

    d. Assuming that all three users are transmitting independently, the probability that all of them are transmitting simultaneously is $(0.1)^3 = .001$. Since the queue only grows when all three users are transmitting, the fraction of time during which the queue grows (which is equal to the probability that all three users are transmitting simultaneously) is .001.

6.   • Link speeds are high, typically at gigabit-per-second rates

    • Direct connections to all other tier-1 ISPs

    • Connected to a large number of tier-2 ISPs

    • International coverage

7.   There is at least one direct link connection between each pair of tier-1 ISPs. Typically, tier-1 ISPs do not charge each other for the traffic sent between them. However, if a tier-2 ISP is directly connected to a tier-1 ISP, the tier-1 ISP charges the tier-2 ISP for the traffic that is sent between the ISPs, thereby forming a provider/customer service relationship.

8.   20 msec; d/s; no; no.

9.   8 msec; L/R; no; no.

10.   The delay is the sum of the transmission delay and propagation delay. More specifically, the total delay is the sum of the time for the sending packet switch to push the packet onto the link and the time for the last bit of the packet to propagate across the link. From Questions 8 and 9, we have 28 msec; $L/R + d/s$.

11.   The first end system requires L/R_1 to transmit the packet onto the first link; the packet propagates over the first link in d_1/s_1; the packet switch adds a processing delay of d_{proc}; after receiving the entire packet, the packet switch requires L/R_2 to transmit the packet onto the second link; the packet propagates over the second link in d_2/s_2. Adding these five delays gives

$$d_{end-end} = L/R_1 + L/R_2 + d_1/s_1 + d_2/s_2 + d_{proc}.$$

To answer the second question, we simply plug the values into the equation to get $8 + 8 + 16 + 4 + 1 = 37$ msec.

12.   Because bits are immediately transmitted, the packet switch does not introduce any delay; in particular, it does not introduce a transmission delay. Thus,

$$d_{end-end} = L/R + d_1/s_1 + d_2/s_2.$$

For the values in Question 11, we get $8 + 16 + 4 = 28$ msec.

13.   The arriving packet must first wait for the link to transmit 3,500 bytes or 28,000 bits. Since these bits are transmitted at 1 Mbps, the queuing delay is 28 msec. Generally, the queuing delay is $[NL + (L - x)]/R$.

14.   The queuing delay is 0 for the first transmitted packet 0, L/R for the second transmitted packet, and, generally, $(n - 1)L/R$ for the nth transmitted packet. Thus, the average delay for the N packets is

$$(L/R + 2L/R + \ldots + (N-1)L/R)/N = L/RN(1 + 2 + \ldots$$
$$+ (N-1)) = LN(N-1)/2RN = (N-1)L/2R$$

Note that here we used the well-known fact that
$$1 + 2 + \ldots + N = N(N+1)/2.$$

15. $L/R = 10$ msec. Thus, we have:

a = 30: I = .3, average queuing delay = (.3/.7) 10 msec = 4.3 msec

a = 60; I = .6, average queuing delay = (.6/.4) 10 msec = 15 msec

a = 90; I = .9, average queuing delay = (.9/.1) 10 msec = 90 msec

a = 99; I = .99, average queuing delay = (.99/.01) 10 msec = 990 msec

The transmission delay for each case is $L/R = 10$ msec. The total delay is the queuing delay plus the transmission delay. For the four cases, this is 14.3 msec, 25 msec, 100 msec, and 1 sec.

16. The roundtrip to router 8 is 13.1 msec and the roundtrip delay to router 9 is 12.7. Two separate roundtrip probes were sent to routers 8 and 9 at two (slightly) different times. During these times, congestion in the links along the path changed. Apparently there was more congestion in at least one of the first eight links during the first probe than in the second probe; hence, the roundtrip delay to router 8 is greater than the roundtrip delay to router 9. The two largest delays occur between routers 3 and 4 and between routers 4 and 5. Routers 3 and 4 appear to be located in Amherst Massachusetts (UMass) and Boston. Routers 4 and 5 appear to be located in Boston and New York City.

17. a. The time required to transmit the packet over one link is $(1 + h)F/R$. The time required to transmit the packet over Q links is $Q(1 + h)F/R$. Thus, the total delay for packet switching is $Q(1 + h)F/R + t_s$.

b. For circuit switching, bits are not "store and forwarded" before each link. Thus, there is only one transmission delay of $F/(R/24) = 24F/R$. The total delay is $24F/R + t_s$.

c. The delay is longer for packet switching when $Q(1 + h)F/R + t_s > 24F/R + t_s$ or equivalently when $Q > 16$. Thus, if there are more than 16 links, packet switching has a larger delay, due to the store and forwarding. If there are fewer than 16 links, circuit switching has a larger delay, due to its reduced transmission rate (R/24).

18. a. application, transport, network, link, physical

b. message, segment, datagram, frame, packet

c. an end-system processes up through the application layer

d. a router processes up through the network layer

e. a link-layer switch processes up through the link layer

The Application Layer

Most Important Ideas and Concepts from Chapter 2

- ◆ **Application-layer protocol.** In Chapter 1 we noted that "*A* protocol *defines the format and the order of messages exchanged between two or more communicating entities, as well as the actions taken on the transmission and/or receipt of a message or other event.*" In chapter 2, we have seen how processes send and receive messages in an application-layer protocol. As a review, identify the messages exchanged and actions taken by the following protocols: HTTP, FTP, DNS, SMTP.

- ◆ **Client/server versus peer-to peer.** These are the two approaches that we studied structuring a network application. In the client/server paradigm (see page 75 of the textbook), a client process requests a service by sending one or more messages to a server process. The server process implements a service by reading the client request, performing some action (for example, in the case of an HTTP server, finding a Web page), and sending one or more messages in reply (in the case of HTTP, returning the requested object). In a peer-to-peer approach, the two ends of the protocol are equals (as in a telephone call).

- ◆ **Two services provided by the Internet's transport layer: reliable, congestion-controlled data transfer (TCP), and unreliable data transfer (UDP).** These are the only services available to an Internet application to transfer data from one process to another remote process. The Internet transport layer does not provide a minimum guaranteed transfer rate, or a bound on the delay from source to destination.

- ◆ **HTTP: request/response interaction.** The HTTP protocol is a simple application-layer protocol. A client (Web browser) makes a request with a GET message, and a Web server provides a reply (see Figure 2.6 on page 89 in your textbook). This is a classical client/server approach. Since HTTP uses TCP to provide reliable transfer of the GET request from client-to-server, and the reply from server-to-client, a TCP connection must be set up. A TCP setup request is sent from the TCP in the client to the TCP in the server, with the TCP server replying to the TCP client. Following this exchange, the HTTP GET message can be sent over the TCP connection from client-to-server, and the reply received (see Figure 2.7 on page 92 in your textbook). With non-persistent HTTP, a new TCP connection must be set up each time the client wants to contact the server. With persistent HTTP, multiple HTTP GET messages can be sent over a single TCP connection, resulting in performance gains from not having to set up a new TCP for each of the HTTP requests beyond the first.

- ◆ **Caching.** Caching is the act of saving a local copy of a requested piece of information (for example, Web document or DNS translation pair) that is retrieved from a distant location, so that if the same piece of information is requested again, it can be retrieved from the local cache, rather than having to retrieve the information again from the distant location. Caching can improve performance by decreasing response time (since the local cache is closer to the requesting client) and avoiding the use of scarce resources (such as the 1.5 Mbps access link shown in Figures 2.11 on page 103 and 2.12 on page 104 in your textbook). Think about ways you use caching in your every day life—e.g., writing a phone number on a piece of paper and keeping it in your pocket, rather than looking it up again in a phone book.

◆ **DNS: core infrastructure implemented as an application-layer process.** The DNS is an application-layer protocol. The name-to-IP-address translation service is performed at the DNS servers, just as any application provides a service to a client via a server. But the DNS service is a very special *network* service—without it the network would be unable to function. Yet it is implemented in very much the same way as any other network application.

◆ **FTP: separate control and data.** Students often ask us why we include an "old" application such as FTP here. FTP is a nice example of a protocol that separates control and data messages. As shown in Figure 2.15 (on page 110 in your textbook), control and data messages are sent over separate TCP connections. This logical and physical separation of control and data (rather than mixing the two types of messages in one connection) helps to make the structure of such an application "cleaner."

◆ **TCP sockets: accept(), and the creation of a new socket.** A "tricky" thing about TCP sockets is that a new socket is created when a TCP server returns from an accept() system call. We call the socket on which the server waits when performing the accept() as a "welcoming socket." The socket returned from the accept() is used to communicate back to the client that connected to the server via the accept() (see Figure 2.28 on page 150 in your textbook).

◆ **UDP sockets: send and pray on the receiving side; datagrams from many senders on the receiving side.** Since UDP provides an unreliable data transfer service, a sender that sends a datagram via a UDP socket has no idea if the datagram is received by the receiver (unless the receiver is programmed to send back a datagram that acknowledges that the original datagram was received). On the receiving side, datagrams from many different senders can be received on the same socket.

◆ **Pull versus push.** How does one application process get data to or from another application process? In a pull system (such as the Web), the data receiver must explicitly request ("pull") the information. In a push system, the data holder sends the information to the receiver without the receiver's explicitly asking for the data (as in SMTP, when an email is "pushed" from sender to receiver).

◆ **Locating information in P2P systems.** We identified three ways to locate information in a P2P system: query flooding, directory systems, and hybrid systems. All existing P2P systems use one of these approaches.

Review Questions

This section provides additional study questions. Answers to each question are provided in the next section.

1. **Client-server, P2P, or Hybrid?** Section 2.1.1 in your textbook discusses three application architectures: client-server, P2P, and a hybrid of the two. Classify each of the scenarios below as client-server, P2P, or hybrid, and explain your answer briefly. Answering these questions may require some Web surfing.

    a. EBay

    b. Skype

    c. BitTorrent

    d. Telnet

    e. DNS

2. **Services provided by the Internet transport protocols.** Indicate whether TCP or UDP (or both or neither) provide the following services to applications:

    a. Reliable data transfer between processes.

    b. Minimum data transmission rate between processes.

    c. Congestion-controlled data transfer between processes.

    d. A guarantee that data will be delivered within a specified amount of time.

    e. Preserve application-level message boundaries. That is, when a sender sends a group of bytes into a socket via a single send operation, that group of bytes will be delivered as a group in a single receive operation at the receiving application.

    f. Guaranteed in-order delivery of data to the receiver.

3. **Fast transactions.** Suppose you want to do a transaction from a remote client to a server as fast as possible, would you use UDP or TCP?

4. **Reliable data transfer with UDP.** Suppose you use UDP to do a transaction from a remote client to a server. UDP provides no reliability, but you want your transaction request to be sent reliably. How could you do is?

5. **Timeliness or in-order delivery.** Suppose that data is being output at a sensor at 1 sample per second. It is important for the receiver to have the most recent value of the sensor's reading, rather than all values (for example, it is better for the receiver to get a current value, rather than an outdated value). Would you use TCP or UDP to send this sensor data? Why?

6. **HTTP basics.** Consider the following string of ASCII characters that were captured by Ethereal when the browser sent an HTTP GET message (this is the

actual content of an HTTP GET message). The characters <cr><lf> are carriage return and line feed characters (that is, the italicized character string <cr> in the text below represents the single carriage-return character that was contained at that point in the HTTP header). Answer the following questions, indicating where in the HTTP GET message below you find the answers.

```
GET /cs453/index.html HTTP/1.1<cr><lf>Host: gai
a.cs.umass.edu<cr><lf>User-Agent: Mozilla/5.0 (
Windows;U; Windows NT 5.1; en-US; rv:1.7.2) Gec
ko/20040804 Netscape/7.2 (ax) <cr><lf>Accept:ex
t/xml,application/xml,application/xhtml+xml,text
/html;q=0.9,text/plain;q=0.8,image/png,*/*;q=0.5
<cr><lf>Accept-Language: en-us,en;q=0.5..Accept-
Encoding: zip,deflate<cr><lf>Accept-Charset: ISO
-8859-1,utf-8;q=0.7,*;q=0.7..Keep-Alive: 300<cr>
<lf>Connection:keep-alive<cr><lf><cr><lf>
```

a. What is the URL of the document requested by the browser? Make sure you give the hostname and the file name parts of the URL.

b. What version of HTTP is the browser running?

c. Is a Netscape or an Internet Explorer browser making the request?

d. Is the browser requesting a non-persistent or a persistent connection?

e. What is the IP address of the computer on which the browser is running?

7. **More HTTP basics.** The text below shows the reply sent from the server in response to HTTPP GET message in Question 6. Answer the following questions, indicating where in the message below you find the answers.

```
HTTP/1.1 200 OK<cr><lf>Date: Tue, 07 Mar 2006
12:39:45GMT..Server: Apache/2.0.52 (Fedora)
<cr><lf>Last-Modified: Sat, 10 Dec 2005 18:27:46
GMT<cr><lf>ETag: "526c3-f22-a88a4c80"<cr><lf>Accept-
Ranges: bytes<cr><lf>Content-Length: 3874<cr><lf>Keep-
Alive: timeout=max=100<cr><lf>Connection: Keep-
Alive<cr><lf>Content-Type: text/html; charset=ISO-8859-
1<cr><lf><cr><lf><!doctype html public "-//w3c//dtd html
4.0 transitional//en"><lf><html><lf><head><lf>  <meta
http-equiv="Content-Type" content="text/html;
charset=iso-8859-1"><lf> <meta name="GENERATOR"
content="Mozilla/4.79 [en] (Windows NT 5.0; U)
Netscape]"><lf>  <title>CMPSCI 453 / 591 / NTU-ST550A
Spring 2005 homepage</title><lf></head><lf> <much more
document text following here (not shown)>
```

    a. Was the server able to find the document successfully or not?

    b. At what time was the document reply provided?

    c. When was the document last modified?

    d. How many bytes are there in the document being returned?

    e. What are the first 5 bytes of the document being returned?

    f. Did the server agree to a persistent connection?

8. **HTTP Performance.** Here, we consider the performance of HTTP, comparing non-persistent HTTP with persistent HTTP. Suppose the page your browser wants to download is 100K bits long, and contains 10 embedded images (with file names img01.jpg, img02.jpg, … img10.jpg), each of which is also 100K bits long. The page and the 10 images are stored on the same server, which has a 300 msec roundtrip time (RTT) from your browser. We will abstract the network path between your browser and the Web server as a 100 Mbps link. You can assume that the time it takes to transmit a GET message into the link is zero, but you should account for the time it takes to transmit the base file and the embedded objects into the "link." This means that the server-to-client "link" has both a 150 msec one-way propagation delay, as well as a transmission delay associated with it. (Review page 39 in the textbook if you are uncertain about the difference between transmission delay and propagation delay.) In your answer, be sure to account for the time needed to set up a TCP connection (1 RTT).

    a. Assuming non-persistent HTTP (and assuming no parallel connections are open between the browser and the server), how long is the *response time*—the time from when the user requests the URL to the time when the page and its embedded images are displayed? Be sure to describe the various components that contribute to this delay.

    b. Again, assume non-persistent HTTP, but now assume that the browser can open as many parallel TCP connections to the server as it wants. What is the response time in this case?

    c. Now assume persistent HTTP (HTTP1.1). What is the response time, assuming no pipelining?

    d. Now suppose persistent HTTP with pipelining is used. What is the response time?

9. **Caching and delays.** Consider the networks shown in the figure below. There are two user machines—m1.a.com and m2.a.com in the network a.com. Suppose the user at m1.a.com types in the URL www.b.com/bigfile.htm into a browser to retrieve a 1Gbit (1000 Mbit) file from www.b.com.

    a. List the sequence of DNS and HTTP messages sent/received from/by m1.a.com, as well as any other messages that leave/enter the a.com network that are not directly sent/received by m1.a.com from the point that the URL is entered into the browser until the file is completely received. Indicate the source and destination of each message. You can assume that every HTTP request by m1.a.com is first directed to the HTTP cache in a.com, that the cache is initially empty, and that all DNS requests are iterated queries.

b. How long does it take to accomplish the steps you outlined in your answer to the previous question regarding the m1a.com HTTP and DNS messages. Explain how you arrived at your answer. In answering this question, you can assume the following:

- The packets containing DNS commands and HTTP commands such as GET are very small compared to the size of the file. Therefore, their transmission times (but not their propagation times) can be neglected.

- Propagation delays within the local area networks (LANs) are small enough to be ignored. The propagation from router R1 to router R2 is 100 msec.

- The one-way propagation delay from anywhere in a.com to any other site in the Internet (except b.com) is 500 msec.

c. Now assume that machine m2.a.com makes a request to the same URL that m1.a.com requested. List the sequence of DNS and HTTP messages sent/received from/by m2.a.com as well as other messages that leave/enter the a.com network that are not directly sent/received by m2.a.com from the point that the URL is entered into the browser until the file is completely received. Indicate the source and destination of each message. (Hint: be sure to consider caching.)

d. Now suppose there is no HTTP cache in network a.com. What is the maximum rate at which machines in a.com can make requests for the file www.b.com/bigfile.htm while keeping the time from when a request is made to when it is satisfied non-infinite in the long run?

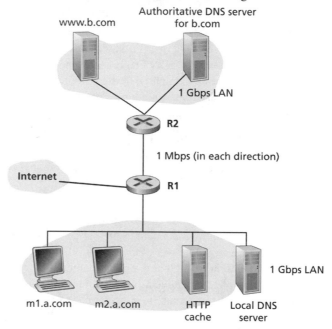

10. **Persistent versus non-persistent TCP connections.** Suppose within your Web browser you click on a link to obtain a Web page. Suppose the IP address for the associated URL is cached in your local host, so that a DNS lookup is not necessary. Denote RTT as the roundtrip time between the local host and the server containing the Web page. Assume the Web page consists of a base HTML file and three small images. Assume the transmission times for all of the objects are negligible in comparison with the RTT. How much time elapses (in terms of RTTs) from when the user clicks on the link until the client receives the entire Web page with each of the following?

a. Non-persistent HTTP with no parallel connections

b. Non-persistent HTTP with up to five parallel connections

c. Persistent HTTP with pipelining

11. **In-band versus out-of band control.** What does it mean when we say that control messages are "in-band"? What does it mean when we say that control messages are "out-of-band"? Give an example of a protocol that has in-band control messages and an example of a protocol that has out of band control messages.

12. **Networking over a slow, short link.** Consider a short (10 meter) link, over which a sender can transmit at a rate of 100 bits/sec in both directions. Suppose that packets containing data are 100Kbits long, and packets containing only control (for example, ACK or handshaking) are 100 bits long. Assume that N parallel connections each get 1/N of the link bandwidth.

    Now consider the HTTP protocol, and suppose that each downloaded object is 100Kbits long, and that the initial downloaded object contains 10 referenced objects from the same sender. Would parallel downloads via parallel instances of non-persistent HTTP make sense in this case? Now consider persistent HTTP. Do you expect significant gains over the non-persistent case? Explain your answer.

13. **Who is sending this packet?** Is the following statement true or false? With UDP sockets, a server can easily determine the IP address of the client, from the data returned via a socket read. Answer the same question (true or false?) for TCP sockets. Briefly explain your answers.

14. **Caching.** Describe two ways in which caching is used in Web access. Describe one way in which caching is used in DNS.

15. **Mail.** What is the difference between the MAIL FROM: in SMTP and From: in the mail message itself?

16. **Push versus pull.** Consider the following forms of non-Internet data distribution: FM radio, broadcast TV, and newspapers. Are these "push" or "pull" systems? Explain. Is the traditional Web browser/server a "push" or "pull" system? Explain. Are there any non-Internet "pull" systems in your life?

17. **Query flooding in P2P networks.** Here, we explore the reverse-path routing of the QueryHit messages in Gnutella. Suppose that Alice issues a Query message. Furthermore, suppose that Bob receives the Query message (which may have been forwarded by several intermediate peers) and has a file that matches the query

    a. Recall that when a peer has a matching file, it sends a QueryHit message along the reverse path of the corresponding Query message. An alternative design would be for Bob to establish a direct TCP connection with Alice and send the QueryHit message over this connection. What are the advantages and disadvantages of such an alternative design?

    b. In the Gnutella protocol, when the peer Alice generates a Query message, it inserts a unique ID in the message's MessageID field. When the peer Bob has a match, it generates a QueryHit message using the same MessageID as the Query message. Describe how peers can use the MessageID field and local routing tables to accomplish reverse-path routing.

    c. An alternative approach, which does not use message identifiers, is as follows. When a query message reaches a peer, before forwarding the message, the peer augments the query message with its IP address. Describe how peers can use this mechanism to accomplish reverse-path routing.

18.   **TCP sockets: accept().** What is the purpose of the connection-oriented welcoming socket, which the server uses to perform an accept()? Once the accept() is done, does the server use the welcoming socket to communicate back to the client? Explain your answer.

19.   **How many port numbers are in use?** Consider incoming TCP and UDP segments arriving at a server, and suppose that (for example, using Ethereal), we see that 150 different destination port numbers are being used. The server acts only as a server (that is, in the socket sense, it does not initiate communication with any other computers as a client; it only responds to incoming segments). Can the number of sockets in use at the server be (a) larger than, (b) equal to, or (c) less than 150? Explain your answer.

20.   **Socket programming.** The skeleton of TCPServer.java is given below. This server receives a sentence from a client on port 6789, capitalizes the sentence, and sends the sentence back to the client. Answer the following questions without looking at the code in the textbook:

   a.   Provide the one line of code that belongs at location (a).

   b.   Provide the one line of code that belongs at location (b).

```
import java.io.*;
import java.net.*;
class TCPServer {
  public static void main(String argv[]) throws Exception
    {
      String clientSentence;
      String capitalizedSentence;
      // (a) Insert line of code
          while(true) {
      // (b) Insert line of code
          BufferedReader inFromClient = new BufferedReader(new
InputStreamReader(connectionSocket.getInputStream()));
    DataOutputStream outToClient = new
DataOutputStream(connectionSocket.getOutputStream());
    clientSentence =
    inFromClient.readLine();
    capitalizedSentence =
    clientSentence.toUpperCase() + '\n';
    outToClient.writeBytes(capitalizedSentence);
          }
    }
}
```

Answers to Review Questions

1. a. EBay is pure client-server application architecture. Ebay is implemented as a Web server (more accurately, a farm of Web servers) that responds to Web client (browser) requests using HTTP.

    b. When two Skype clients talk to each other, they do so as peers. However, in order to locate a peer, a Skype client will first contact a directory server in a client-server manner. Therefore, Skype has a hybrid application architecture.

    c. BitTorrent is a pure P2P application architecture. It is interesting because it will concurrently download different pieces of a file from different peers.

    d. Telnet is a pure client-server application architecture. The client is the process that contacts the Telnet server (at port 23 to allow remote login on the remote machine where the Telnet server process is running).

    e. DNS is a pure client-server application architecture. The DNS client is the process that sends the DNS REQUEST message (to port 53 at the DNS server); the server is the DNS server process that replies with a DNS REPLY message.

2. a. TCP provides a reliable byte-stream between client and server.

    b. Neither

    c. TCP

    d. Neither

    e. UDP preserves message boundaries, while TCP is byte-stream oriented, and does not preserve message boundaries.

    f. TCP will deliver bytes to the receiver in the order in which they were sent. UDP does not guarantee delivery of message data in the order in which they were sent.

3. You would use UDP. With UDP, the transaction can be completed in one roundtrip time (RTT)—the client sends the transaction request into a UDP socket, and the server sends the reply back to the client's UDP socket. With TCP, a minimum of two RTTs are needed—one to set-up the TCP connection, and another for the client to send the request, and for the server to send back the reply.

4. You would build reliability into your application. This could be done, for example, by having the client re-transmit its request if it doesn't hear back from the server within a certain amount of time. We will cover techniques to provide reliable data transfer in Chapter 3.

5. You would use UDP. With TCP, data (even old data) will be sent again and again until it is received correctly. Moreover, since data is passed up in order

by the TCP receiver, newer data will not be delivered to the receiving application until all old data has been delivered to the application. With UDP, if data is lost, newer data will eventually be sent and received, without waiting for the lost data to be recovered.

6. a. The document request was http://gaia.cs.umass.edu/cs453/index.html. The `Host:` field indicates the server's name and `/cs453/index.html` indicates the file name.

   b. The browser is running HTTP version 1.1, as indicated just before the first `<cr><lf>` pair.

   c. A Netscape browser is making the request. The `User-agent:` field indicates "Mozilla," which is a nickname for Netscape's browser.

   d. The browser is requesting a persistent connection, as indicated by the `Connection:keep-alive`.

   e. This is a trick question. This information is not contained in an HTTP message anywhere. So there is no way to tell this from looking at the exchange of HTTP messages alone. One would need information from the IP datagrams (that carried the TCP segment that carried the HTTP GET request) to answer this question.

7. a. The status code of `200` and the phrase `OK` indicate that the server was able to locate the document successfully.

   b. The reply was provided on Tuesday, 07 Mar 2006 12:39:45 Greenwich Mean Time.

   c. The document index.html was last modified on Saturday, 10 Dec 2005 18:27:46 GMT.

   d. There are 3874 bytes in the document being returned.

   e. The first five bytes of the returned document are: `<!doc`.

   f. The server agreed to a persistent connection, as indicated by the `Connection: Keep-Alive` field.

8. a. For starters, note that it takes 1 msec to send 100K bits over a 100 Mbps link. The delays associated with this scenario are:

   • 300 msec (RTT) to set up the TCP connection that will be used to request the base file.

   • 150 msec (one way delay) to send the GET message for the base file, and have the message propagate to the server, plus 1 msec to transmit the base file, plus 150 msec for the base file to propagate back to the client (for a total of 301 msec).

   • 300 msec (RTT) to set up TCP connection that will be used to request the img.01.jpg file.

   • 150 msec (one way delay) to send the GET message for img01.jpg and have it propagate to the server, plus 1 msec to transmit the img01.jpg file, plus 150 msec for the img01.jpg file to propagate back to the client (for a total of 301 msec).

The last two steps above are repeated for the nine image files img02.jpg through img10.jpg. The total response time is therefore $300 + 11 \times 601$, or 6.911 seconds.

b. • 300 msec (RTT) to set up the TCP connection that will be used to request the base file.

 • 150 msec (one way delay) to send the GET message for the base file, and have the message propagate to the server, plus 1 msec to transmit the base file, plus 150 msec for the base file to propagate back to the client (for a total of 301 msec).

 • The client now sets up 10 parallel TCP connections. 300 msec (RTT) is needed to set up the 10 TCP connections (since they are set up in parallel).

 • 150 msec (one way delay) to send the 10 GET messages in parallel for img01.jpg through img10.jpg and have the GET messages propagate to the server. It will take the server 10 msec to transmit the 10 jpeg files, plus 150 msec for the last jpeg file to propagate back to the client (for a total of 310 msec).

Putting this all together, the response time is
$$300 + 301 + 300 + 310 = 1.211 \text{ seconds.}$$

c. • 300 msec (RTT) to set up the TCP connection that will be used to request the base file, and 10 images.

 • 150 msec (one way delay) to send the GET message for the base file, and have the message propagate to the server, plus 1 msec to transmit the base file, plus 150 msec for the base file to propagate back to the client (for a total of 301 msec).

 • 150 msec (one way delay) to send the GET message for img01.jpg and have it propagate to the server, plus 1 msec to transmit the img01.jpg file, plus 150 msec for the img01.jpg file to propagate back to the client (for a total of 301 msec).

The last step above is repeated for the nine image files img02.jpg through img10.jpg. The total response time is therefore
$$300 + 11 \times 301 = 3.611 \text{ seconds}$$

d. • 300 msec (RTT) to set up the TCP connection that will be used to request the base file, and 10 images.

 • 150 msec (one way delay) to send the GET message for the base file, and have the message propagate to the server, plus 1 msec to transmit the base file, plus 150 msec for the base file to propagate back to the client (for a total of 301 msec).

- 150 msec (one way delay) to send the 10 GET messages serially for img01.jpg through img10.jpg and have the GET messages propagate to the server (recall that we are assuming the GET message has zero transmission time). It will take the server 10 msec to transmit the 10 jpeg files, plus 150 msec for the last jpeg file to propagate back to the client (for a total of 310 msec).

The total response time is $300 + 301 + 310 = 911$ msec.

9.   a.   - m1.a.com needs to resolve the name www.b.com to an IP address so it sends a DNS REQUEST message to its local DNS resolver.

- The local DNS server does not have any information so it contacts a root DNS server with a REQUEST message.

- The root DNS server returns name of DNS Top Level Domain server for .com.

- The local DNS server contacts the .com TLD.

- The TLD .com server returns the authoritative name server for b.com.

- The local DNS server contacts the authoritative name server for b.com.

- The authoritative name server for b.com returns the IP address of www.b1.com.

- The HTTP client sends a HTTP GET message to www.b1.com, which is redirected by the client browser to the HTTP cache in the a.com network.

- The HTTP cache does not find the requested document in its cache, so it sends the GET request to www.b.com.

- www.b.com receives the GET request and sends the file from www.b.com to R2.

- The 1 Gbit file is transmitted over the 1 Mbps link between R2 and R1 to the HTTP cache.

- The 1 Gbit file is sent from the HTTP cache to m1.a.com.

b.   Let $t = 0$ be the time at which the user enters www.b.com into the browser

- The HTTP client will send its HTTP GET message to www.b1.com through the local HTTP cache in a.com. This takes no time given the assumptions above.

- The HTTP cache does not find the requested document in its cache. Therefore it must request the document from b.com. Before it can send a GET request to www.b.com, it must find out the IP address for www.b.com. To do this, it will have to use the DNS. To resolve the name www.b.com to an IP address, the Web cache sends a DNS RE-QUEST message to its local DNS resolver. This takes no time given the assumptions above.

- The local DNS server does not have any information so it contacts a root DNS server with a REQUEST message. This takes .5 sec given the assumptions above. At $t = 500$ msec, the root DNS server receives the message.

- The root DNS server returns the name of the DNS Top Level Domain server for .com. This takes 500 msec given the assumptions above. At $t = 1$ sec, the local DNS server receives the message and now knows the address of the .com TLD DNS server.

- The local DNS server contacts the .com TLD DNS server. This takes 500 msec given the assumptions above. At $t = 1.5$, the TLD DNS server receives the message.

- The TLD .com server returns the authoritative DNS server for b.com. This takes 500 msec given the assumptions above. At $t = 2$, the local DNS server receives the message.

- The local DNS server contacts the authoritative name server for b.com. This takes 100 msec given the assumptions above. At $t = 2.1$, the authoritative DNS server for b.com receives the message.

- The authoritative name server for b.com returns the IP address of www.b1.com. This takes 100 msec, given the assumptions above. At $t = 2.2$, the local DNS server for a.com receives the message, and returns this message to the HTTP Web cache.

- The Web cache is now ready to request the document from www.b.com. It takes 200 msec to set up the TCP connection between the HTTP cache and www.b.com.

- At $t = 2.4$ sec, the Web cache sends the GET request to www.b.com. It takes 100 msec for the GET request to propagate to www.b.com, given the assumptions above.

- At $t = 2.5$ sec, www.b.com receives the GET request and immediately begins sending the file in reply. If we assume that as soon as the first bit reaches R2, it is forwarded over the link between R2 and R1, then this transmission delay can be ignored, since the transmission of the file from www.b.com is pipelined with the transmission of the file between R2 and R1.

- The 1 Gbit file must be transmitted over the 1 Mbps link between R2 and R1. This takes 1,000 seconds. There is an additional 100 msec propagation delay. Thus, at $t = 1002.6$ secs, the last bit of the file is received at R1. If we assume that R1 forwards packets to the HTTP cache as it receives them from R2, then the transmission delay between R1 and the cache can be ignored since it is pipelined with the transmission from R2 to R1.

- There is a 1 sec delay to send the 1 Gbps file from R1 to the HTTP cache. If we assume that as soon as the first few bits of the file arrive at the router, they are forwarded to the cache, then this delay can be ignored.
- There is a 1 sec delay to send the 1 Gbps file from the HTTP cache to m1.a.com. If we assume that as soon as the first few bits of the file arrive at the cache, they are forwarded to the m1.a.com, then this delay can be ignored.

Thus, the total delay is approximately 1002.6 seconds.

c.
- The HTTP client at m2.a.com will send its HTTP GET message to www.b1.com through the local HTTP cache in a.com. This takes no time given the assumptions above.
- The HTTP cache finds the requested document in its cache, so it sends a GET request with an If-Modified-Since to www.b.com. This takes 100 msec given the assumptions above. Note that the cache does not need to contact the DNS, assuming it has cached the IP address associated with www.b.com.
- www.b.com receives the GET request. The document has not changed, so www.b.com sends a short HTTP REPLY message to the HTTP cache in a.com indicating that the cached copy is valid. (This takes 100 msec given the assumptions.)
- There is a 1 sec delay to send the 1 Gbps file from the HTTP cache to m2.a.com.

Thus, the total delay is: .1 + .1 + 1 = 1.2 sec.

d. Since it takes approximately 1000 sec to send the file from R2 to R1, the maximum rate at which requests to send the file from b.com to a.com is 1 request every 1000 seconds, or an arrival rate of .001 requests/sec.

10. a. 2 RTT to get each image: 4(2 RTT) = 8 RTT
    b. 2 RTT for base, 2 RTT for remaining three images: 4 RTT
    c. 2 RTT for base; 1 RTT for remaining three images: 3 RTT

11. When we say that control messages are "in-band," it means that control message and data messages may be interleaved with each other on the same connection. A single message may contain both control information and data. When we say that control messages are "out-of-band," it means that control and data messages are carried on separate connections. HTTP, DNS, and SMTP have in-band control, while FTP has out-of-band control messages.

12. Parallel download would only share the 100K bandwidth among the 10 connections (each getting just 10K bits/sec) thus, there is no significant advantage here. With persistent HTTP we avoid the SYN and SYNACK exchange, but that only requires 2 seconds (1 second to send the 100 bit SYN message

over the 100 bps link, and 1 second to receive the ACK). Given that each object takes 101 seconds to send and receive the ACK, the use of pipelining gives only a 2 percent gain.

13. This is true for UDP since the UDP packet (i.e., the Datagram Packet data structure returned from the ServerSocket.read( ) call) contains the IP address of the sender of the UDP packet. This is false for a TCP socket since the socket only returns the byte stream sent by the client, but no identifying information about the client.

14. A Web browser will cache objects locally in its browser cache. An institution might also have a Web cache, which each browser contacts to satisfy its Web requests. If the requested Web page is not in the Web cache, the Web cache will request and receive the object from the origin server, cache the object locally (in case some other browser requests the object), and return the object to the request browser. When the local DNS gets a translation request for a name that it is not in its cache, it will obtain the name/address translation pair and then cache this value so that future requests for translating the same name can be satisfied by the local DNS server, without going out to the larger DNS system.

15. The MAIL FROM: in SMTP is a message from the SMTP client that identifies the sender of the mail message to the SMTP server. The From: on the mail message itself is NOT an SMTP message, but rather is just a line in the body of the mail message.

16. FM radio, broadcast TV, and newspapers are all push systems. Information is sent out via these media regardless of whether or not anyone is tuning in to the TV or radio stations, or buying the newspaper. Also, content is not individualized for the receiver. The Web is a pull system because data is not transmitted to the browser unless it is explicitly requested by the browser. Some automated phone response systems are non-Internet pull systems. For example, I may call a number to get my horoscope, and enter my birth date in order to have my horoscope read to me.

17. a. The advantage of sending the QueryHit message directly over a TCP connection from Bob to Alice is that the QueryHit message is routed by the underlying Internet without passing through intermediate peers; thus, the delay in sending the message from Bob to Alice should be substantially less. The disadvantage is that each peer that has a match would ask Alice to open a TCP connection; Alice may therefore have to opens tens or hundreds of TCP connections for a given query.

    b. When a QueryHit message enters a peer, the peer records the MessageID in a table along with an identifier of the TCP socket from which the message arrived. When the same peer receives a QueryHit message with the same MessageID, it indexes the table and determines the socket to which it should forward the message.

    c. As the query message propagates through peers, each peer includes its IP address in the query message, creating a list of IP addresses. When there is a query match, the peer with the match includes the list in the Query-Hit message. When a peer receives a QueryHit, it finds the preceding node in the list and forwards the message to that preceding peer.

18. The welcoming socket is used in a server to wait for incoming client connection requests in connection-oriented (TCP-based) communication. A new socket is created on return from the accept( ). This new socket is then used by the server to communicate back to the client.

19. If all traffic is UDP, then the number of sockets will equal the number of ports. If there is TCP traffic, then the number of sockets will be greater, because each welcoming socket, and the socket created as a result of accept( )ing a connection will have the same destination port number.

20. See page 155 of your textbook.

Transport Layer

Most Important Ideas and Concepts from Chapter 3

- **Logical communication between two processes.** Application processes use the logical communication provided by the transport layer to send messages to each other, free from the worries of the details of the network infrastructure used to carry these messages. Whereas a transport-layer protocol provides logical communication between processes, a network-layer protocol provides logical communication between hosts. This distinction is important but subtle; it is explained on page 186 of the textbook with a cousin/house analogy. An application protocol lives only in the end systems and is not present in the network core. A computer network may offer more than one transport protocol to its applications, each providing a different service model. The two transport-layer protocols in the Internet—UDP and TCP—provide two entirely different service models to applications.

- **Multiplexing and demultiplexing.** A receiving host may be running more than one network application process. Thus, when a receiving host receives a packet, it must decide to which of its ongoing processes it is to pass the packet's payload. More precisely, when a transport-layer protocol in a host receives a segment from the network layer, it must decide to which socket it is to pass the segment's payload. The mechanism of passing the payload to the appropriate socket is called *demultiplexing*. At the source host, the job of gathering data chunks from different sockets, adding header information (for demultiplexing at the receiver), and passing the resulting segments to the network layer is called *multiplexing*.

- **Connectionless and connection-oriented demultiplexing.** Every UDP and TCP segment has a field for a source port number and another field for a destination port number. Both UDP (connectionless) and TCP (connection-oriented) use the values in these fields—called port numbers—to perform the multiplexing and demultiplexing functions. However, UDP and TCP have important, but subtle differences in how they do multiplexing and demultiplexing. In UDP, each UDP socket is assigned a port number, and when a segment arrives at a host, the transport layer examines the destination port number in the segment and directs the segment to the corresponding socket. On the other hand, a TCP socket is identified by the four-tuple: (source IP address, source port number, destination IP address, destination port number). When a TCP segment arrives from the network to a host, the host uses all four values to direct (demultiplex) the segment to the appropriate socket.

- **UDP.** The Internet (and more generally TCP networks) makes available two transport-layer protocols to applications: UDP and TCP. UDP is a no-frills, bare-bones protocol, allowing the application to talk almost directly with the network layer. The only services that UDP provides (beyond IP) is multiplexing/demultiplexing and some light error checking. The UDP segment has only four header fields: source port number, destination port number, length of the segment, and checksum. An application may choose UDP for a transport protocol for one or more of the following reasons: it offers finer application control of what data is sent in a segment and when; it has no connection establishment; it has no connection state at servers; and it has less packet header overhead than TCP. DNS is an example of an application protocol that uses UDP. DNS sends its queries and answers within UDP segments, without any connection establishment between communicating entities.

♦ **Reliable data transfer.** Recall that, in the Internet, when the transport layer in the source host passes a segment to the network layer, the network layer does not guarantee it will deliver the segment to the transport layer in the destination host. The segment could get lost and never arrive at the destination. For this reason, the network layer is said to provide *unreliable data transfer.* A transport-layer protocol may nevertheless be able to guarantee process-to-process message delivery even when the underlying network layer is unreliable. When a transport-layer protocol provides such a guarantee, it is said to provide *reliable data transfer* (*RDT*). The basic idea behind reliable data transfer is to have the receiver acknowledge the receipt of a packet; and to have the sender retransmit the packet if it does not receive the acknowledgement. Because packets can have bit errors as well as be lost, RDT protocols are surprisingly complicated, requiring acknowledgements, timers, checksums, sequence numbers, and acknowledgement numbers.

♦ **Pipelined reliable data transfer.** The textbook incrementally develops an RDT *stop-and-wait* protocol in Section 3.4. In a stop-and-wait protocol, the source sends one packet at a time, only sending a new packet once it has received an acknowledgment for the previous packet. Such a protocol has very poor throughput performance, particularly if either the transmission rate, R, or the round-trip time, RTT, is large. In a pipelined protocol, the sender is allowed to send multiple packets without waiting for an acknowledgment. Pipelining requires an increased range in sequence numbers and additional buffering at sender and receiver. The textbook examined two pipelined RDT protocols in some detail: Go-Back-N (GBN) and Selective Repeat (SR). Both protocols limit the number of outstanding unacknowledged packets the sender can have in the pipeline. GBN uses cumulative acknowledgments, only acknowledging up to the first non-received packet. A single-packet error can cause GBN to retransmit a large number of packets. In SR, the receiver individually acknowledges correctly received packets. SR has better performance than GBN, but is more complicated, both at sender and receiver.

♦ **TCP.** TCP is very different from UDP. Perhaps the most important difference is that TCP is reliable (it employs a RDT protocol) whereas UDP isn't. Another important difference is that TCP is connection oriented. In particular, before one process can send application data to the other process, the two processes must "handshake" with each other by sending to each other (a total of) three empty TCP segments. The process initiating the TCP handshake is called the *client.* The process waiting to be hand-shaken is the *server.* After the 3-packet handshake is complete, a connection is said to be established and the two processes can send application data to each other. A TCP connection has a send buffer and a receive buffer. On the send side, the application sends bytes to the send buffer, and TCP grabs bytes from the send buffer to form a segment. On the receive side, TCP receives segments from the network layer, deposits the bytes in the segments in the receive buffer, and the application reads bytes from the receive buffer. TCP is a byte-stream protocol in the sense that a segment may not contain a single application-layer message. (It may contain, for example, only a portion of a message or contain multiple messages.) In order to set the timeout in its RDT protocol, TCP uses a dynamic RTT estimation algorithm.

TCP's RDT service ensures that the byte stream that a process reads out of its receive buffer is exactly the byte stream that was sent by the process at the other end of the connection. TCP uses a pipelined RDT with cumulative acknowledgments, sequence numbers, acknowledgment numbers, a timer, and a dynamic timeout interval. Retransmissions at the sender are triggered by two different mechanisms: timer expiration and triple duplicate acknowledgments.

♦ **Flow control.** Because a connection's receive buffer can hold only a limited amount of data, there is the danger that the buffer overflows if data enters the buffer faster than it is read out of the buffer. Many transport protocols, including TCP, use flow control to prevent the occurrence of buffer overflow. The idea behind flow control is to have the receiver tell the sender how much spare room it has in its receive buffer; and to have the sender restrict the amount of data that it puts in the pipeline to be less than the spare room. Flow control speeds matching: it matches the sender's send rate to the receiver's read rate.

♦ **Congestion control principles.** Congestion has several costs. Large queuing delays occur as the packet arrival rate nears the link capacity. Unneeded retransmissions by the sender in the face of large delays cause routers to use their link bandwidth to forward unneeded copies of packets. And, when a packet is dropped along a path, the transmission capacity that was used at each of the upstream links to forward that packet (up to point at which it is dropped) is wasted.

♦ **TCP congestion control.** Because the IP layer provides no explicit feedback to end systems regarding network congestion, TCP uses end-to-end congestion control rather than network-assisted congestion control. The amount of data a TCP connection can put into the pipe is restricted by the sender's congestion window. The congestion window essentially determines the send rate. Unlike the simpler GBN and SR protocols covered in Section 3.4, this window is dynamic. TCP reduces the congestion window during the occurrence of a loss event, where a loss event is either a timeout or the receipt of three duplicate acknowledgements. When loss events are not occurring, TCP increases its congestion window. This gives rise to the sawtooth dynamics for the congestion window, as shown in Figure 3.50 on page 267 of the textbook. The exact rules for how the loss events influence the congestion window are determined by three mechanisms: Additive Increase Multiplicative Decrease (AIMD); slow start; and fast retransmit.

Review Questions

This section provides additional study questions. Answers to each question are provided in the next section.

1. **Logical communication between processes.** Suppose the network layer provides the following service. The source host accepts from the transport layer a segment of maximum size 1,000 bytes and a destination host address. The network layer then guarantees delivery of the segment to the transport layer at the destination host. Suppose many network application processes can be running at the destination host.

   a. Design the simplest possible transport layer protocol that will get application data to the desired process at the destination host. Assume the operating system in the destination host has assigned a two-byte port number to each running application process.

   b. Modify this protocol so that it provides a "return address" to the destination process.

   c. In your protocols, does the transport layer "have to do anything" in the core of the computer network?

2. **Logical communication between families.** Consider a planet where everyone belongs to a family of five, every family lives in its own house, each house has a unique address, and each person in a house has a unique name. Suppose this planet has a mail service that delivers letters from source house to destination house. The mail service requires that (i) the letter be in an envelope and that (ii) the address of the destination house (and nothing more) be clearly written on the envelope. Suppose each family has a delegate family member who collects and distributes letters for the other family members. The letters do not necessarily provide any indication of the recipients of the letters.

   a. Using the solution to Question 1 as inspiration, describe a protocol that the delegates can use to deliver letters from a sending family member to a receiving family member.

   b. In your protocol, does the mail service ever have to open the envelope and examine the letter in order to provide its service?

3. **UDP demultiplexing.** Suppose a process in host C has a UDP socket with port number 787. Suppose host A and host B each send a UDP segment to host C with destination port number 787. Will both of these segments be directed to the same socket at host C? If so, how will the process at host C know that these segments originated from two different hosts?

4. **UDP and TCP checksum.**

   a. Suppose you have the following two bytes: 00110101 and 01101001. What is the 1s complement of these two bytes?

b.   Suppose you have the following two bytes: 11110101 and 01101001. What is the 1s complement of these two bytes?

c.   For the bytes in part a), give an example where one bit is flipped in each of the two bytes and yet the 1s complement doesn't change.

5.   **TCP multiplexing.** Suppose that a Web server runs in host C on port 80. Suppose this Web server uses persistent connections, and is currently receiving requests from two different hosts: A and B. Are all of the requests being sent through the same socket at host C? If they are being passed through different sockets, do both of the sockets have port 80? Discuss and explain.

6.   **Why choose UDP?** An application may choose UDP for a transport protocol because UDP offers finer application control (than TCP) of what data is sent in a segment and when it is sent.

a.   Why does an application have more control of what data is sent in a segment?

b.   Why does an application have more control of when the segment is sent?

7.   **A simple synchronized message exchange protocol.** Consider two network entities: A and B, which are connected by a perfect bi-directional channel (that is, any message sent will be received correctly; the channel will not corrupt, lose, or re-order packets). A and B are to deliver data messages to each other in an alternating manner: first A must deliver a message to B, then B must deliver a message to A, then A must deliver a message to B, and so on. Draw a FSM specification for this protocol (one FSM for A and one FSM for B). Don't worry about a reliability mechanism here; the main point is to create a FSM specification that reflects the synchronized behavior of the two entities. You should use the following events and actions, which have the same meaning as protocol rdt1.0, shown on page 204 of the textbook:

```
rdt_send(data), packet = make_pkt(data),
udt_send(packet), rdt_rcv(packet), extract (packet,data),
deliver_data(data).
```

Make sure that your protocol reflects the strict alternation of sending between A and B. Also, be sure to indicate the initial states for A and B in your FSM description.

8.   **Adding ACKs to the simple synchronized message exchange protocol.** Let's modify the protocol in Question 7: After receiving a data message from the other entity, an entity should send an explicit acknowledgement back to the other side. An entity should not send a new data item until after it (i) has received an ACK for its most recently sent message, (ii) has received a data message from the other entity, and (iii) ACKed that message received from the other entity. Draw the FSM specification for this modified protocol. You may use the new function that was introduced in protocol rdt2.0, shown on

page 206 in the textbook: udt_send(ACK). You may want to use (but do not have to, depending on your solution) the following event as well: rdt_rcv(rcvpkt) && isACK(rcvpkt), which indicates the receipt of an ACK packet (as in rdt2.0 in the textbook), and rdt_rcv(rcvpkt) && is-DATA(rcvpkt), which indicates the receipt of a data packet.

9. **A simple three-node synchronized message exchange protocol.** Consider three network entities: A, B, and C, which are connected by perfect point-to-point bi-directional channels (that is, any message sent will be received correctly; the channel will not corrupt, lose, or re-order packets). A, B, and C are to deliver data messages to each other in a rotating manner: first A must deliver a message to B, then B must deliver a message to C, and then C must deliver a message to A, and so on. Draw a FSM specification for this protocol (one FSM for A, one for B, and one for C). You should use the same events as in Questions 7 and 8, except that the udtsend() function now includes the name of the recipient. For example, udt_send(data,B) is used to send a message to B. Your protocol does *not* have to use ACK messages.

10. **A final variation on the simple synchronized message exchange protocol.** Consider (yet again!) two network entities: A and B, which are connected by a bi-directional channel that is perfect (that is, any message sent will be received correctly; the channel will not corrupt, lose, or re-order packets). A and B are to deliver data messages to each other in the following manner: A is to send *two* messages to B, and then B is to send one message to A. Then the cycle repeats. You should use the same events as in the questions above. Your protocol does *not* have to use ACK messages. (The key idea is to think about how to use states to track how many messages A has sent: one or two.)

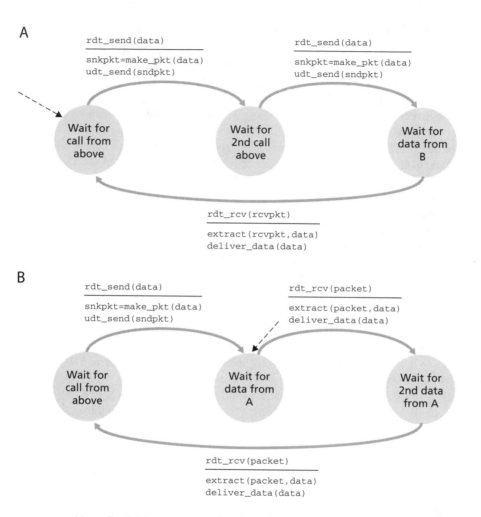

11. **Reliable data transfer.** Recall the NAK-free `rdt` protocol in the textbook (figure 3.13) for a channel with bit errors (but without packet loss). The FSM protocol is shown below. How many states does the receiver need: 1, 2, or 4? What are these states? Without looking at the textbook, draw the FSM for the corresponding receiver. (Hint: the receiver must now include the sequence number of the packet being acknowledged.)

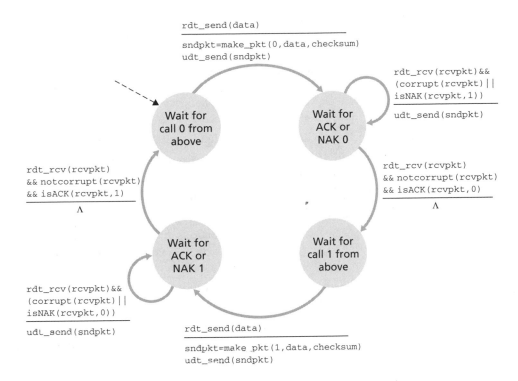

12. **Designing a minimalist data transfer protocol.** Chapter 3 shows a number of mechanisms used to provide for reliable data transfer:

- checksum
- ACKs
- timers
- sequence numbering

Consider a sender and receiver that are connected by a sender-to-receiver channel that can corrupt and lose packets. The receiver-to-sender channel is perfect (that is, it will not lose or corrupt packets). The delay on each channel is known to always be less than some maximum value, *d*. Neither channel will reorder packets. (Note: re-read the channel properties just described and make sure you understand them!) Design a reliable data transfer protocol for this scenario *using only those mechanisms (among the four listed above) that are absolutely required.* That is, if you use a mechanism that is not required, you will not receive full credit, even if the protocol works. Your protocol should be as simple as possible but have the functionality to deliver data reliably under the stated assumptions. Your solution does not need to be efficient; it must work correctly.

a. Draw the sender and receiver FSMs.

b. For each of the mechanisms (from among the four listed above) that you use in your protocol, explain the role/purpose of the mechanism and why you cannot get by without it. (Note: this does not imply that your protocol will use all four mechanisms above—maybe it does; maybe it does not. However, you must explain why you need the mechanisms that you have chosen to include.)

13. **Pipelined reliable data transfer.** Recall the Go-back-N protocol in Section 3.4.

a. Does this protocol have a timer for each unacknowledged packet?

b. When a timer expires, what happens?

c. Use the interactive applet for Go-Back-N and quickly try to generate seven packets. How many packets did you generate? Just after attempting to generate the seven packets, pause the animation and kill the first packet. What happens when the timeout expires?

14. **Pipelined reliable data transfer with selective repeat.** Recall the selective repeat protocol in Section 3.4.

a. Does this protocol have a timer for each unacknowledged packet?

b. When an acknowledgement arrives for the oldest unacknowledged packet, what happens?

15. **Can a window size be too large for the sequence number space?** Consider the Go-Back-N protocol. Suppose that the size of the sequence number space (number of unique sequence numbers) is N, and the window size is N. Show (give a timeline trace showing the sender, receiver, and the messages they exchange over time) that the Go-Back-N protocol will not work correctly in this case.

16. **TCP sequence numbers.** Host A and B are communicating over a TCP connection, and Host B has already received from A all bytes up through byte 144. Suppose that Host A then sends two segments to Host B back-to-back. The first and second segments contain 20 and 40 bytes of data, respectively. In the first segment, the sequence number is 145, source port number is 303, and the destination port number is 80. Host B sends an acknowledgement whenever it receives a segment from Host A.

a. In the second segment sent from Host A to B, what are the sequence number, source port number, and destination port number?

b. If the first segment arrives before the second segment, in the acknowledgement of the first arriving segment, what is the acknowledgment number, the source port number, and the destination port number?

c. If the second segment arrives before the first segment, in the acknowledgement of the first arriving segment, what is the acknowledgment number?

d. Suppose the two segments sent by A arrive in order at B. The first acknowledgement is lost and the second segment arrives after the first timeout interval, as shown in the figure below. Complete the diagram, showing all other segments and acknowledgements sent. (Assume there is no additional packet loss.) For each segment you add to the diagram, provide the sequence number and number of bytes of data; for each acknowledgement that you add, provide the acknowledgement number.

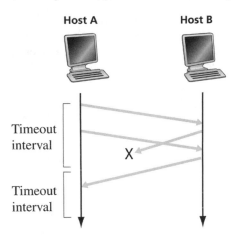

17. **Round-trip time estimation.** Let $\alpha = 0.2$. Suppose for a given TCP connection three acknowledgments have been returned with RTTs: RTT for first ACK = 80 msec; RTT for second ACK = 60 msec; and RTT for third ACK = 100 msec. Determine the value of EstimatedRTT after each of the three acknowledgments.

18. **Flow control.** Host A and B are directly connected with a 100 Mbps link. There is one TCP connection between the two hosts, and Host A is sending an enormous file to Host B over this connection. Host A can send application data into the link at 50 Mbps but Host B can read out of its TCP receive buffer at a maximum rate of 10 Mbps. Describe the effect of TCP flow control.

19. **TCP connection management.**

a. A server process in Host B has a welcoming socket at port 977. What will trigger the server process to create a connection socket? What is the source IP address and source port number for this connection socket?

b. How many bytes is a TCP SYN segment? What flags are set in a TCP SYN segment?

c. What must happen for Host B to complete this connection?

20. **TCP congestion control.** Consider sending a large file from one host to another over a TCP connection that has no loss.

a. Suppose TCP uses AIMD for its congestion control without slow start. Assuming CongWin increases by 1 MSS every time an ACK is received and assuming approximately constant round-trip times, how long does it take for CongWin to increase from 1 MSS to 5 MSS (assuming no loss events and constant RTT)?

b. What is the average throughput (in terms of MSS and RTT) for this connection up through time = 4 RTT?

21. **More TCP congestion control.** Suppose that in TCP, the sender window is of size N, the base of the window is at sequence number x, and the sender has just sent a complete window's worth of segments. Let RTT be the sender-to-receiver-to-sender round-trip time, and let MSS be the segment size.

a. Is it possible that there are ACK segments in the receiver-to-sender channel for segments with sequence numbers lower than x? Justify your answer.

b. Assuming no loss, what is the throughput (in packets/sec) of the sender-to-receiver connection?

c. Suppose TCP is in its congestion avoidance phase. Assuming no loss, what is the window size after the N segments are ACKed?

22. **TCP Potpourri.**

a. Consider two TCP connections, one between Hosts A (sender) and B (receiver), and another between Hosts C (sender) and D (receiver). The RTT between A and B is half that of the RTT between C and D. Suppose that the senders' (A's and C's) congestion window sizes are identical. Is their throughput (number of segments transmitted per second) the same? Explain.

b. Now suppose that the *average* RTT between A and B, and C and D are identical. The RTT between A and B is constant (never varies), but the RTT between C and D varies considerably. Will the TCP timer values of the two connections differ, and if so, how are they different, and why are they different?

c. Give one reason why TCP uses a three-way (SYN, SYNACK, ACK) handshake rather than a two-way handshake to initiate a connection.

d. It is said that a TCP connection "probes" the network path it uses for available bandwidth. What does this mean?

e. What does it mean when we say that TCP uses "cumulative acknowledgement"? Give two reasons why cumulative acknowledgment is advantageous over selective acknowledgment.

Answers to Review Questions

1. a. Call this protocol Simple Transport Protocol (STP). At the sender side, STP accepts from the sending process a chunk of data not exceeding 998 bytes, a destination host address, and a destination port number. STP adds a two-byte header to each chunk and puts the port number of the destination process in this header. STP then gives the destination host address and the resulting segment to the network layer. The network layer delivers the segment to STP at the destination host. STP then examines the port number in the segment, extracts the data from the segment, and passes the data to the process identified by the port number.

    b. The segment now has two header fields: a source port field and a destination port field. At the sender side, STP accepts a chunk of data not exceeding 996 bytes, a destination host address, a source port number, and a destination port number. STP creates a segment that contains the application data, source port number, and destination port number. Then it gives the segment and the destination host address to the network layer. After receiving the segment, STP at the receiving host gives the application process the application data and the source port number.

    c. No, the transport layer does not have to do anything in the core; the transport layer "lives" in the end systems.

2. a. For sending a letter, the family member is required to give the delegate the letter itself, the address of the destination house, and the name of the recipient. The delegate clearly writes the recipient's name on the top of the letter. Then the delegate puts the letter in an envelope and writes the address of the destination house on the envelope. Then the delegate gives the letter to the planet's mail service. At the receiving side, the delegate receives the letter from the mail service, takes the letter out of the envelope, and notes the recipient name written at the top of the letter. Then the delegate gives the letter to the family member with this name.

    b. No, the mail service does not have to open the envelope; it only examines the address on the envelope.

3. Yes, both segments will be directed to the same socket. For each received segment, at the socket interface, the operating system will provide the process with the IP address of the host that sent the segment. The process can use the supplied IP addresses to determine the origins of the individual segments.

4. a. Adding the two bytes gives 10011110. Taking the 1s complement gives 01100001.

    b. Adding the two bytes gives 01011111. The 1s complement gives 10100000.

    c. First byte = 00110001; second byte = 01101101.

5.   For each persistent connection, the Web server creates a separate "connection socket." Each connection socket is identified with a four-tuple: (source IP address, source port number, destination IP address, destination port number). When Host C receives an IP datagram, it examines these four fields in the datagram/segment to determine to which socket it should pass the payload of the TCP segment. Thus, the requests from A and B pass through different sockets. The identifier for both of these sockets has 80 for the destination port; however, the identifiers for these sockets have different values for the source IP addresses. Unlike UDP, when the transport layer passes a TCP segment's payload to the application process, it does not specify the source IP address, as this is implicitly specified by the socket identifier.

6.   a. Consider sending an application message over a transport protocol. With TCP, the application writes data to the connection's send buffer and TCP will grab bytes without necessarily putting a single message in the TCP segment; TCP may put more or less than a single message in a segment. UDP, on the other hand, encapsulates in a segment whatever the application gives it; so that, if the application gives UDP an application message, this message will be the payload of the UDP segment. Thus, with UDP, an application has more control of what data is sent in a segment.

    b. With TCP, due to flow control and congestion control, there may be significant delay from the time when an application writes data to its send buffer until when the data is given to the network layer. UDP does not have delays due to flow control and congestion control.

7.

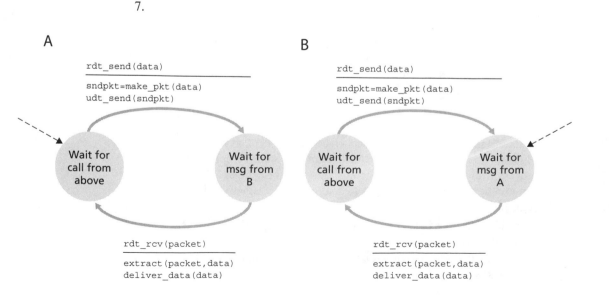

8.

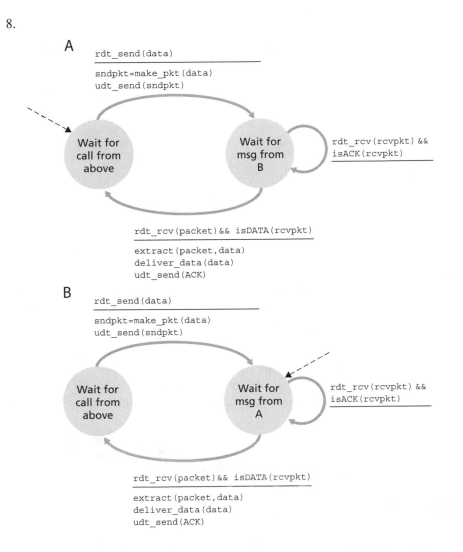

In the solution above, we've used the isACK(rcvpkt) and isDATA(rcvpkt) expressions to indicate whether an ACK or DATA message has been received. If we add another state to each FSM, which is used to reflect whether the entity is waiting for an ACK or waiting for DATA, then we do not need to use these expressions. Below is an alternate solution (for A only; B is similar) that does not use these expressions. The solution above and the solution below are equally good, they differ only in how they represent the handling of the received message. Indeed, they are FSMs for the same protocol!

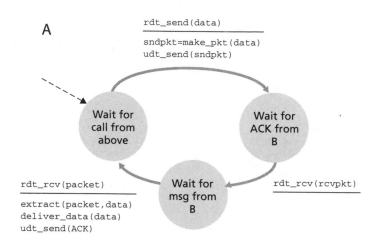

9. The answer to this question is essentially the same as for the first of these FSM questions, except that we need to indicate the address of the outgoing message. Because we have specified that the channels are point-to-point, A does not see any communication between B and C. Thus, A only needs to send its message to B, and then wait for a message from C before sending another message to B. The FSM for A is shown below. (Note that if we had specified that the channel connecting the entities was a broadcast channel, then we would have had to consider the fact that A was receiving messages sent from B to C, which A would receive but then would have to ignore.)

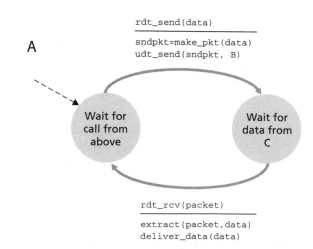

10.

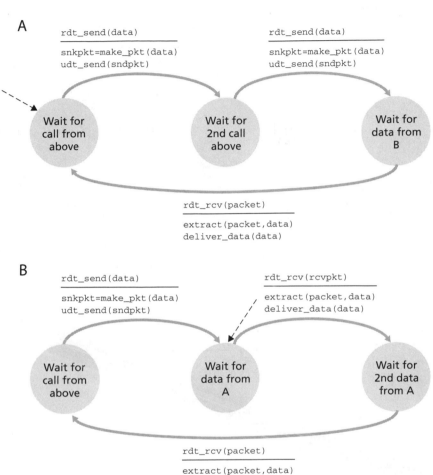

11.   This protocol needs two states: wait for zero from below; wait for one from below. The FSM for the receiver is given below.

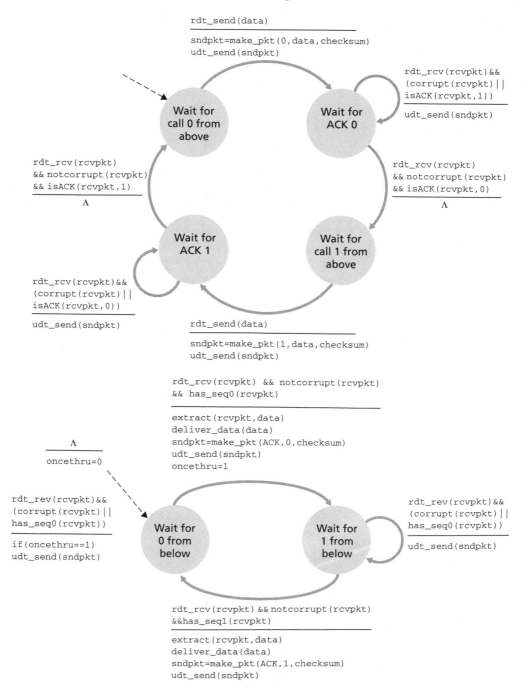

12.   a.

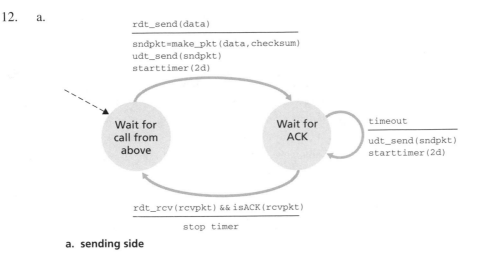

```
                    rdt_send(data)
                    _____

                    sndpkt=make_pkt(data,checksum)
                    udt_send(sndpkt)
                    starttimer(2d)
```

```
                                                                timeout
                                                                _____
         Wait for                    Wait for
         call from                     ACK                     udt_send(sndpkt)
         above                                                 starttimer(2d)
```

```
                    rdt_rcv(rcvpkt) && isACK(rcvpkt)
                    _____

                            stop timer
```

a. sending side

```
         Wait for
         call from
         below
```

```
                    rdt_rcv(rcvpkt) && notcorrupt(rcvpkt)
                    _____

                    extract(rcvpkt,data)
                    deliver_data(data)
                    udt_send(sndpkt)
```

b. receiving side

b.   Because the sender-to-receiver channel can corrupt packets, the data sent
     on the sender-to-receiver channel will need a *checksum* to detect bit errors.
     Because the sender-to-receiver channel can lose packets, we will need to
     have a *timer* to timeout and retransmit packets that have not been received
     by the receiver. The receiver will need to indicate which packets it has re-
     ceived by using an ACK *message*; if a packet is not received or is received
     corrupted, no ACK is sent. Because the maximum delay of the channel is
     bounded at, d the sender can set its timeout value to $2d$, and therefore only
     retransmit when it is certain that a retransmission is needed (and expected
     by the receiver). Thus, there is no need for sequence numbers, since there
     will be no unneeded (and unexpected at the receiver) retransmissions. .

13. a. No, GBN has only one timer, for the oldest unacknowledged packet.

b. When the timer expires, the sender resends all packets that have been sent but have not yet been acknowledged.

c. The applet only generates six packets since the window size is six. The sender doesn't receive an acknowledgment for previously unacknowledged data before the timer expires. When the timer expires, the sender resends all six packets.

14. a. Yes, there is a timer for each unacknowledged packet.

b. The window advances. If the sender has another packet to send, it sends the packet and starts a timer for the packet.

15. Suppose that the sequence number space is 0,1 and N = 2, that is, that two messages can be transmitted but not yet acknowledged. The timeline below shows an error that can occur.

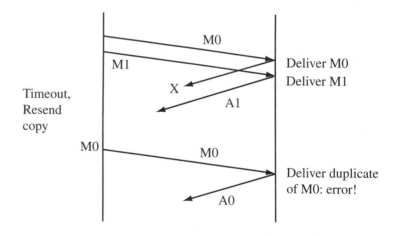

16. a. The first and second segments contain 20 and 40 bytes of data, respectively. In the second segment sent from A to B, the sequence number is 165, the source port number is 303, and the destination port number is 80.

b. The first acknowledgment has acknowledgment number 165, source port 80, and destination port 303.

c. The acknowledgment number will be 145, indicating that it is still waiting for bytes 145 and onward.

d. The sequence number of the retransmission is 145 and it carries 20 bytes of data. The acknowledgment number of the additional acknowledgment is 205.

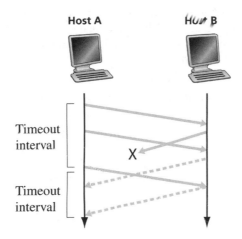

17. After the first ACK, the EstimatedRTT is equal to the RTT associated with the ACK, namely, 80 msec. After the second ACK, we use the following formula:

$$\text{EstimatedRTT} = (1 - \alpha)\,\text{EstimatedRTT} + \alpha\,\text{SampleRTT}$$

to obtain:

$$\text{EstimatedRTT} = (0.8)(80\text{ msec}) + (0.2)(60\text{ msec}) = 76\text{ msec}$$

Similarly, after third ACK, we get

$$\text{EstimatedRTT} = (0.8)(76\text{ msec}) + (0.2)(100\text{ msec}) = 71.2\text{ msec}$$

18. Host A sends data into the receive buffer faster than Host B can remove data from the buffer. The receive buffer fills up at a rate of roughly 40 Mbps. When the buffer is full, Host B signals to Host A to stop sending data by setting RcvWindow = 0. Host A then stops sending until it receives a TCP segment with RcvWindow > 0. Host A will thus repeatedly stop and start sending as a function of the RcvWindow values it receives from Host B. On average, the long-term rate at which host A sends data to host B as part of this connection is no more than 10 Mbps.

19. a. When Host B receives a TCP SYN segment with destination port number 977, the operating system at Host B will create a (half-open) connection socket. The TCP SYN packet has a source port number, which becomes the source port number of the socket. The TCP SYN segment is also contained in an IP datagram, which has a source IP address, which in turn becomes the source IP address for the socket.

b. A TCP SYN packet contains no data and is thus 20 bytes. In a SYN segment, the SYN flag is set, but not the ACK flag.

c. After receiving the SYN packet, the server sends to the client on Host B a SYNACK segment, which is also 20 bytes, and which has both the SYN and ACK flags set. The client then sends an ACK packet back to the server. Upon receiving this ACK packet, the connection is fully open at both the client and server sides.

20. a. It takes 1 RTT to increase CongWin to 2 MSS; 2 RTTs to increase to 3 MSS; 3 RTTs to increase to 4 MSS; and 4 RTTs to increase to 5 MSS.

b. In the first RTT 1 MSS was sent; in the second RTT 2 MSS were sent; in the third RTT 3 MSS were sent; in the fourth RTT 4 MSS were sent. Thus, up to time 4 RTT, $1 + 2 + 3 + 4 = 10$ MSS were sent (and acknowledged). Thus, one can say that the average throughput up to time 4 RTT was (10 MSS)/(4 RTT) = 2.5 MSS/RTT.

21. a. It is possible. Suppose that the window size is $N = 1$. The sender sends packet $x - 1$, which is delayed and so it timeouts and retransmits $x - 1$. There are now two copies of $x - 1$ in the network. The receiver receives the first copy of $x - 1$ and ACKs. The receiver then receives the second copy of $x - 1$ and ACKs. The sender receives the first ACK and sets its window base to x. At this point, there is still an ACK for $x - 1$ propagating back to the sender.

b. Assume that N is measured in segments. The sender can thus send N segments, each of size MSS bytes every RTT sec. The throughput is $N \cdot MSS/RTT$.

c. $N + 1$

22. a. No. The two sessions will transmit the same number of segments per RTT. But since the RTT of the A-B connection is half that of the other session, its throughput will be twice as large.

b. The TCP timer takes the estimate of the RTT and adds on a factor to account for the variation in RTTs. Therefore, the C-D connection timeout value will be larger.

c. Suppose a client transmits multiple SYN messages that take a long time to be received at the server, so the client terminates (thinking the server is dead). The server then accepts these SYN connections (with only a two-way handshake, the server needs to commit as soon as the SYN is received). However, the client side is no longer present, so the server now has multiple connections opened with no client on the other side.

d. TCP's sawtooth behavior results from TCP continuing to increase its transmission rate until it congests some link in the network (that is, until there is no unused bandwidth on that link) at which point a loss occurs. TCP then backs off and continues to increase its bandwidth again.

e. An acknowledgement of X in TCP tells the sender that all data up to X has been correctly received. Cumulative ACKs can decrease the amount of ACK overhead. For example, a TCP receiver will wait a short time before ACKing in the hope that the next in-sequence packet will arrive, and then will just generate a single ACK (for the second packet), which will acknowledge both packets. Also even if the receiver separately ACKs packets X and X + 1, if the ACK of X is lost but the ACK of X + 1 is received, the sender will know that X was received by the receiver.

The Network Layer

Most Important Ideas and Concepts from Chapter 4

♦ **Routing protocols: link-state and distance vector.** It's often said that the network layer is all about routing, and there's a lot of truth in that statement. In Chapter 4 we cover two basic approaches to routing: *link-state* and *distance vector*. In the link-state approach, all nodes *broadcast* their link-state information (the existence of links to neighbors and the links' costs) to all nodes in the network, giving all nodes a common global view of the network's topology. Each node then runs a shortest path algorithm (such as Dijkstra's algorithm) using this network topology to determine the least-cost path from itself to all other nodes in the network. Packets are then routed along these least-cost paths. Distance vector algorithms are distributed in nature—each node communicates only with its directly-connected neighbors, exchanging its estimates of its least cost to reach each node in the network. For routing purposes, a node also maintains the identity of the first-hop (directly-connected) neighbor along the least cost path to each destination. Through an iterative process of (i) pairwise exchange of distance vectors; (ii) recomputation of least cost paths given new distance vector information received from neighbors; and (iii) transmission of new distance vector information to neighbors if a node's estimates of its least cost to a destination has changed, the distance vector algorithm converges to a set of distance vectors for which each node has its own least cost to each destination, and the next-hop neighbor along that least cost path. Note that with distance vector algorithms, a node does not know the entire least cost path from source to destination; however, each node along the way knows the identity of the next node along this least cost path. Note also that neither link-state nor distance vector algorithms necessarily route along least congested paths (unless link costs reflect the current congestion state of a link).

♦ **Inter-AS versus Intra-AS routing.** Link-state and distance vector algorithms conceptually consider a flat (non-hierarchical) network topology. Internet routing, however, has a distinct two-level hierarchy based on the notion of an autonomous system—a network that is under the control of a single organization. When routing *within* an autonomous system (intra-AS routing), the organization can choose its own routing algorithm; RIP, OSPF, or IS-IS are popular choices. When routing *among* autonomous systems (inter-AS routing), each AS can be considered as a single node in an AS graph, with the inter-AS routing algorithm determining how packets are routed among ASs. BGP is the (only) inter-AS routing algorithm in use in the Internet. For this reason, BGP is sometimes referred to as the "glue" that binds the Internet.

♦ **Service models for the network layer.** Students often find the discussion of the network-layer service model (or service models in general) to be boring. But the idea of the network service model, which defines the end-end packet delivery service that will be provided to the transport layer, is nonetheless extremely important. We have seen that the Internet adopts a best-effort model, in which no guarantees are made at the network layer regarding how long it will take for a datagram to reach its destination, or whether the datagram will even make it to its destination in the first place.

♦ **Datagrams and virtual circuits.** Datagrams and virtual circuits represent the two major approaches to network layer service that have been taken over the years. The Internet is a datagram network, in which each network-layer datagram carries the IP address of the final destination of the datagram. This address is used by a router in forwarding the datagram toward its final destination. In a virtual circuit (VC) network, each packet of data (called a "cell" in ATM VC networks) carries a VC number, which is used by a switch in forwarding the packet of data toward its destination. In a VC network, when a call is made between a source and destination, a call setup procedure is needed to create state in each switch on the end-to-end path that matches the VC number for this call with the outgoing switch port to which the VC's packets of data will be forwarded. Similarly, a call-teardown procedure is needed in VC networks.

♦ **Forwarding versus routing.** Forwarding and routing are two of the main functions of a network layer. *Forwarding* refers to the per-router action of moving a packet arriving at an input port to the appropriate output port. In a datagram network, the output port is determined by looking up the arriving datagram's destination in a forwarding table, and using a longest-prefix matching algorithm to find the entry that contains the identity of the output port to which the arriving datagram should be forwarded; in a VC network, this is done by looking up the VC of the arriving unit of data in the VC lookup table. *Routing* refers to the process of determining the end-to-end path that a packet will take through the network. We studied both link-state and distance vector routing algorithms.

♦ **Addressing.** Perhaps the only network-layer topic that students think is more boring than service models is addressing. But understanding Internet addressing is absolutely crucial to understanding how the network layer works! Everyone knows that the IP address is 32-bits long, and is often represented in dotted-decimal notation. More importantly, the addresses assigned to Internet devices (consisting of a network part and a host part) deeply reflect the structure of the network. Figure 4.16 on page 333 of the textbook shows that all hosts on the same subnet must have the same network part of their address; in Chapter 5 we will see that this ability to determine whether or not a destination is on the same network (in an IP addressing sense) will be used to determine whether a datagram can be sent directly to its final destination over the single network (in an IP addressing sense) that directly connects the two nodes, or whether the datagram must be forwarded to an intervening router. As we saw in Figure 4.18 on page 336 of the textbook, the structure of the addresses within an AS also allows for route aggregation, allowing a BGP router to advertise an address prefix that is common to nodes in the AS.

♦ **Delay and loss within a router.** In Chapters 1 through 3, we made many references to datagrams being lost or delayed within the network. In Section 4.3 (specifically,

Section 4.3.4), where we explore the inner structure of a router, we see that queuing delay and loss occur at the router's input and output ports. At the output port, queuing occurs because packets arrive to the output port at a rate that is faster than the outgoing link rate; hence, a queue of packets awaiting transmission begins to grow, and packet delay increases. If the memory used to hold queued packets becomes full, arriving packets will be dropped, or a packet will be dropped from the queue to make room for an arriving packet. At an input port, a queue will form when the rate at which the switching fabric is able to forward packets to the output ports is less than the rate of incoming packets to that input port.

♦ **Border Gateway Protocol (BGP).** We noted above that BGP is the *only* protocol used to route datagrams among autonomous systems, and thus it is the "glue" that binds the Internet together. We saw that BGP allows an autonomous system to choose which path it uses to reach a destination. Indeed, that is a local policy decision that is left to the network manager. More importantly, an autonomous system can also control which routes it advertises to its neighbors; this too is a local policy decision. For example, if an AS advertised no routes, then none of its neighbors would route any traffic to that AS. Of course, an AS that receives no incoming traffic isn't very useful!

♦ **Tunneling.** In Figure 4.24 on page 350 in the textbook, we see that tunneling can be used to connect two routers logically over a path that contains multiple routers. This allows two Ipv6 routers to exchange IPv6 datagrams with each other, via routers that only "speak" IPv4. This is done by having the router at the source end of the tunnel encapsulate the IPv6 datagram within an IPv4 datagram, and address the IPv4 datagram to the IPv4 address for the destination side of the tunnel; the upper-layer-protocol field is set to type 41 to indicate to the destination side of the tunnel that the IPv4 datagram contains an IPv6 datagram. When the destination end of the tunnel receives an IP datagram addressed to itself, with a protocol number of 41, it recognizes that this is an IPV6-within-IPv4 datagram, extracts the IPv6 datagram, and forwards the IPv6 datagram on as needed.

♦ **The IP datagram.** The message here is plain and simple: all networking students really should know what an IPv4 datagram looks like (see Figure 4.13 on page 326 of the textbook). While it may not be exciting, like broccoli it is "good for you." Actually, there are not *that* many fields, and the meaning/use of each of the fields is fairly straightforward. Students are seldom asked to memorize all of the fields, but a favorite exam question is to ask students to describe five or six fields.

Review Questions

This section provides additional study questions. Answers to each question are provided in the next section.

1. **Virtual circuit and datagram networks.** Identify three important differences between a virtual circuit network (for example, ATM) and a datagram network (for example, Internet).

2. **Virtual circuits.** Consider Figure 4.3 on page 308 of the textbook and the virtual circuit (VC) table for router R1 shown above the figure. Write the set of VC table entries in router R2 in Figure 4.3 that are needed to ensure that the VC tables in R1 and R2 are consistent, that is, that the VCs entering/leaving interface 2 in router R1 are consistent with the VCs leaving/entering interface 1 in router R2.

3. **IP addressing.**
   a. Write the IP address 129.17.129.97 in its binary form.
   b. Consider an IP subnet with prefix 129.17.129.97/27. Provide the range of IP addresses (of form xxx.xxx.xxx.xxx to yyy.yyy.yyy.yyy) that can be assigned to this subnet.
   c. Suppose an organization owns the block of addresses of the form 129.17.129.97/27. Suppose it wants to create four IP subnets from this block, with each block having the same number of IP addresses. What are the prefixes (of form xxx.xxx.xxx/y) for the four IP subnets?

4. **IP datagram.** Suppose a host has a file consisting of 2 million bytes. The host is going to send this file over a link with an MTU of 1,500 bytes. How many datagrams are required to send this file?

5. **IP fragmentation.** Consider sending a 2,000-byte datagram into a link with a MTU of 980 bytes. Suppose the original datagram has the identification number 227. How many fragments are generated? For each fragment, what is its size, what is the value of its identification, fragment offset, and fragment flag?

6. **Longest prefix matching.** Consider a datagram network using 32-bit host addresses. Suppose that a router has three interfaces, numbered 0 through 2, and that packets are to be forwarded to these link interfaces as follows. Any address not within the ranges in the table below should not be forwarded to an outgoing link interface. Create a forwarding table using longest prefix matching.

Destination address range	Outgoing link interface
00000000 00000000 00000000 00000000 through 00000001 11111111 11111111 11111111	0
01010101 00000000 00000000 00000000 through 01010101 11111111 11111111 11111111	1
01010110 00000000 00000000 00000000 through 01010111 11111111 11111111 11111111	2

7. **Longest prefix matching.** Consider the same datagram network using 32-bit host addresses, and a router that has three interfaces, numbered 0 through 2 (see Question 6). Packets are to be forwarded to these link interfaces as follows. The address ranges for the first, third, and fourth entries in the table below are the same as in Question 6; the second entry below is new. Any address not within the ranges in the table below should not be forwarded to an outgoing link interface.

Destination address range	Outgoing link interface
00000000 00000000 00000000 00000000 through 00000001 11111111 11111111 11111111	0
00000000 00000000 10000000 00000000 through 00000000 00000000 11111111 11111111	2
01010101 00000000 00000000 00000000 through 01010101 11111111 11111111 11111111	1
01010110 00000000 00000000 00000000 through 01010111 11111111 11111111 11111111	2

8. **Longest prefix matching.** Consider the same datagram network using 32-bit host addresses, and a router that has three interfaces, numbered 0 through 2 (see Question 7). Packets are to be forwarded to these link interfaces as follows. The address ranges for the second and third entries in the table below are the same as in the earlier problem; the first entry below has an upper-end of the address range that is smaller than before. Any address not within the ranges in the table below should not be forwarded to an outgoing link interface.

Destination address range	Outgoing link interface
00000000 00000000 00000000 00000000 through 00000001 10000000 00000000 00000000	0
01010101 00000000 00000000 00000000 through 01010101 11111111 11111111 11111111	1
01010110 00000000 00000000 00000000 through 01010111 11111111 11111111 11111111	2

9. **IP addressing.** Consider the network shown below. Each of the subnets A-D contains at most 30 hosts; subnet E connects routers R1 and R2.

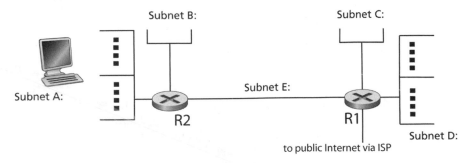

a. Assign network addresses to the five subnets shown above (that is, write the addresses you have assigned).

b. Suppose that there are 17 hosts in A–D. Does your answer to Question 9a) change? If so why or why not?

c. What is the network prefix advertised by router R1 to the public Internet?

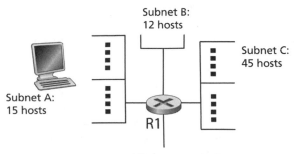

10. **IP addressing.**

    a. Consider an Internet address of the form 129.19.40.0/23. What does the /23 signify?

    b. Consider the network shown above, consisting of a single router, R1, with three subnets A, B and C, with 15, 12, and 45 hosts respectively on these subnets. Assign an address range to the hosts in subnets A, B, and C so that only a single aggregated address needs to be advertised by R1 to the public Internet, and that the size of the advertised aggregated address range is minimized. In a sentence or two, explain how you arrived at your answer.

11. **NAT.** Consider the scenario shown in Figure 4.20 on page 340 of the textbook. Suppose that host 10.0.0.2 initiates a connection, using source port 5500 to a Web server listening at port 80 at 128.119.40.186.

    a. Complete the NAT translation table for this TCP connection.

    b. What are the source and destination IP addresses and port numbers on the IP datagram arriving to the WAN side of the router with interface address 138.76.29.7?

12. **Tunneling.** How does the router at the destination end of a tunnel (see Figure 4.24 on page 350 of the textbook) know that the IPv4 datagram contains an IPv6 datagram that it should extract from the IPv4 packet?

13. **Dijkstra's (link-state) algorithm.** Consider the network shown below. Show the operation of Dijkstra's (link-state) algorithm for computing the least cost path from D to all destinations. What is the shortest path from D to B, and what is the cost of this path?

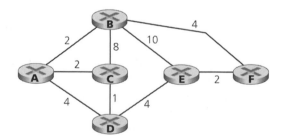

14. **Dijkstra's (link-state) algorithm (more).** Consider the network shown in Question 13. Show the operation of Dijkstra's (link-state) algorithm for computing the least cost path from E to all destinations. What is the shortest path from E to B, and what is the cost of this path?

15. **Dijkstra's (link-state) algorithm (even more).** Consider the network shown in Question 14. Show the operation of Dijkstra's (link-state) algorithm for computing the least cost path from B to all destinations. What is the shortest path from B to D, and what is the cost of this path?

16. **Distance vector algorithm.** Consider the network below.

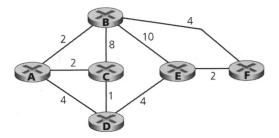

a. What are A, B, C, D, E, and F's distance vectors? Note: you do not have to run the distance vector algorithm; you should be able to compute distance vectors by inspection. Recall that a node's distance vector is the vector of the least cost paths from itself to each of the other nodes in the network.

b. Now consider node C. From which other nodes does C receive distance vectors?

c. Consider node C again. Through which neighbor will C route its packets destined to E? Explain how you arrived at your answer, given the distance vectors that C has received from its neighbors.

d. Consider node E. From which other nodes does E receive distance vectors?

e. Consider node E again. Through which neighbor will E route its packets destined to B. Explain how you arrived at your answer, given the distance vectors that E has received from its neighbors.

17. **Distance vector algorithm (more).** Consider the network below.

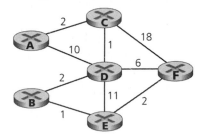

a. What are A, B, C, D, E, and F's distance vectors? Note: you do not have to run the distance vector algorithm; you should be able to compute distance vectors by inspection. Recall that a node's distance vector is the vector of the least cost paths from itself to each of the other nodes in the network.

b. Consider node C. From which other nodes does C receive distance vectors?

c. Consider node C again. Through which neighbor will C route its packets destined to F? Explain how you arrived at your answer, given the distance vectors that C has received from its neighbors.

d. Consider node B. From which other nodes does E receive distance vectors?

e. Consider node B again. Through which neighbor will B route its packets destined to C? Explain how you arrived at your answer, given the distance vectors that B has received from its neighbors.

18. **Distance vector algorithm (even more).** Consider the network below.

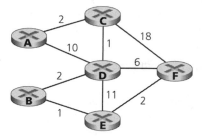

a. What are the initial distance vectors in A, C, D and F, before the distance vector algorithm begins executing?

b. Suppose that node A sends its distance vector to C (and that no other distance vectors are exchanged). What are the distance vectors in A, C, D, and F?

c. Suppose that node D sends its distance vector to C (and that no other distance vectors are exchanged). What are the distance vectors in A, C, D, and F?

19. **BGP.** Consider the network below in which network W is a customer of ISP A, network Y is a customer of ISP B, and network X is a customer of both ISPs A and C.

a. What BGP routes will A advertise to X?

b. What routes will X advertise to A?

c. What routes will A advertise to C? For each answer provide a one-sentence explanation.

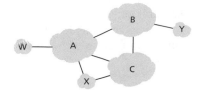

20. **Minimum spanning tree.** Consider the network shown below and find the minimum spanning tree that connects all nodes.

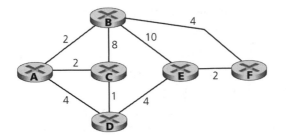

21. **Minimum spanning tree.** Consider the network from Question 20. Find the set of shortest paths from all nodes to A (and indicate these paths in the graph using thicker shaded lines). Then, using arrows like those shown in Figure 4.41 on page 388 of the textbook, indicate the links over which packets will be forwarded using reverse path forwarding, and the links over which packets will not be forwarded, given that node A is the source.

Answers to Review Questions

1. a. A virtual circuit requires call setup.

   b. A virtual circuit has call teardown.

   c. In a VC network, a packet carries a VC ID rather than a destination address.

   d. Resources can be allocated to a call/connection in a VC network (typically during call setup).

2. A partial VC table for R2 is shown below. Note that for incoming interface 1, there must be entries for VC numbers 22 and 17, since the VC table for R1 (shown on page 308 of the textbook) has entries for outgoing interface 2, with VC numbers 22 and 17 (and interface 2 in R1 is connected to interface 1 in R2). Similarly, since interface 2 in R1 has an incoming VC number 63, R2 must have a VC with outgoing VC number 63 on R2 interface 1.

Incoming interface	Incoming VC number	Outgoing interface	Outgoing VC number
1	22		
1	17		
		1	63

3. a. 10000001 00010001 10000001 01100001

   b. 10000001 00010001 10000001 01100000 to 10000001 00010001 10000001 01111111 or equivalently, 129.17.129.96 to 129.17.129.127

   c. There are 32 addresses in the range; we give 8 addresses to each block; thus, 129.17.129.96 to 129.17.129.103, 129.17.129.104 to 129.17.129.111, 129.17.129.112 to 129.17.129.119, and 129.17.129.120 to 129.17.129.127.

4. Assume the data is carried in TCP segments, with each TCP segment also having 20 bytes of header. Then each datagram can carry $1,500 - 40 = 1460$ bytes of the file as follows:

$$\text{Number of datagrams required} = \left\lceil \frac{2 \times 10^6}{1460} \right\rceil = 1370.$$

All but the last datagram will be 1,500 bytes; the last datagram will be $1,260 + 40 = 1,300$ bytes. Note that the host creates datagrams and not fragments.

5. The maximum size of data field in each fragment $= 960$ (20 bytes IP header). Thus, the number of required fragments

$$= \left\lceil \frac{2000 - 20}{960} \right\rceil = 3$$

Each fragment will have identification number 227. Each fragment except the last one will be of size 980 bytes (including IP header). The last data-gram will be of size 80 bytes (including IP header). The offsets of the three fragments will be 0,120, 240. The first two fragments will have flag = 1; the last fragment will have flag = 0.

6.

Prefix	Outgoing link interface
0000000	0
01010101	1
0101011	2

Since all addresses beginning with 0000000 are routed to interface 0, all addresses beginning with 0101010101 are forwarded to interface 1, and all addresses beginning 0101011 are forwarded to interface 2, we only need a single table entry for these interfaces.

7.

Prefix	Outgoing link interface
0000000	0
00000000 00000000 1	2
01010101	1
0101011	2

Because of the longest prefix matching rule, all addresses beginning with 0000000 00000000 1 are now forwarded to interface 2, while all other addresses beginning with 00000000 are forwarded to interface 0. The forwarding for prefixes 01010101 and 0101011 are the same as before.

8.

Prefix	Outgoing link interface
00000000	0
00000001 0	0
00000001 10000000 00000000 00000000	0
01010101	1
0101011	2

The tricky part of this question is to make sure that no packets with addresses higher than 00000001 10000000 00000000 00000000 are routed to interface 0.

9. a. Each subnet needs to address up to 30 hosts, using the rightmost 5 bits of the address. The five subnet addresses are thus x.y.z.000/27, x.y.z.001/27, x.y.z.010/27, x.y.z.011/27, and x.y.z.100/27, where we have shown the first three binary digits of the last byte of the addresses explicitly. More properly, these addresses are x.y.z.0/27, x.y.z.32/27, x.y.z.64/27, x.y.z.96/27, and x.y.z.128/27 in dotted decimal notation. Other answers with different bit values in bits 25, 26, and 27 are also possible, as long as the five three-bit patterns used are unique.

   b. The answer stays unchanged. In order to address 17 hosts, 5 bits are still needed, and so the network part of the address will be 27 bits long again.

   c. x.y.z./24

10. a. The /23 signifies that the network part of the host address is the leftmost 23 bits.

   b. Subnet A requires at least 4 bits of addressing, subnet B requires at least 4 bits of addressing, and subnet C requires at least 6 bits of addressing. Let the first 3 bytes of the address for all of the hosts be X.Y.Z.

   - The address for hosts in subnet C are in the range X.Y.Z.00CCCCCC, where the last byte of the address begins with two 0's and the rest of the 6 bits are used to address hosts in C. Note that the second bit in the last byte is a 0. For subnets A and B, this bit will be a 1.

   - The address for hosts in subnet B are in the range X.Y.Z.010BBBBB. The last byte of the address begins with 010 and the final 5 bits can be used to address the hosts in B.

   - The address for hosts in subnet A are in the range X.Y.Z.011AAAAA. The last byte of the address begins with 011 (which differs from the leading 010 for subnet B, and the leading 00 for subnet C) and the final 5 bits can be used to address the hosts in A.

   The size of the single aggregated network that is advertised is thus X.Y.Z.0/25—the last seven bits are used to address hosts in subnets A, B, and C.

11. a.

NAT translation table	
WAN side	LAN side
138.76.29.7, 5002	10.0.0.2, 5500

   Note that the use of 5002 on the WAN side is arbitrary. The NAT box will simply use an unused port number.

   b. For the datagram returning from the Web sever: source IP: 128.119.40.186, source port: 80, dest. IP: 138.76.29.7, dest. Port: 5002.

12. First, since the IPv4 datagram is addressed to the router at the destination end of the tunnel, that router knows it must do something with that IPv4 datagram when it arrives (after all, it is the destination of the IPv4 datagram!). The upper-layer protocol field value in the IPv4 datagram tells the router that the IPv4 datagram contains an encapsulated IPv6 datagram (just as this upper-layer protocol field value is used to indicate that the IP datagram contains a TCP or UDP segment).

13.

N	D(A),p(A)	D(B),p(B)	D(C),p(C)	D(E),p(E)	D(F),p(F)
D	4,D	infty	1,D	4,D	infty
DC	3,C	9,C		4,D	infty
DCA		5,A		4,D	infty
DCAE		5,A			6,E
DCAEB					6,E

The shortest path from D to B is D C A B. The cost of this path is 5.

14.

N	D(A),p(A)	D(B),p(B)	D(C),p(C)	D(D),p(D)	D(F),p(F)
E	infty	10,E	infty	4,E	2,E
EF	infty	6,F	infty	4,E	
EFD	8,D	6,F	5,D		
EFDC	7,C	6,F			
EFDCB	7C				

The shortest path from E to B is E F B. The cost of this path is 6.

15.

N	D(A),p(A)	D(C),p(C)	D(D),p(D)	D(E),p(E)	D(F),p(F)
B	2,B	8,B	infty	10,B	4,B
BA		4,A	8,A	10,B	4,B
BAC			5,C	10,E	4,B
BACF			5,C	6,E	
BACFD				6,E	

The shortest path from B to D is B A C D. The cost of this path is 5.

16.   a.

node	Destination					
	A	B	C	D	E	F
A	0	2	2	3	7	6
B	2	0	4	5	6	4
C	2	4	0	1	5	7
D	3	5	1	0	4	6
E	7	6	5	4	0	2
F	6	4	7	6	2	0

b.   From its neighbors, nodes A, B, and D. Note that C does not receive distance vectors from nodes E and F, since they are not direct neighbors.

c.   See page 358 in the textbook for notation.

   C's cost to E via B is $c(C,B) + D_B(E) = 8 + 6 = 14$

   C's cost to E via A is $c(C,A) + D_A(E) = 2 + 7 = 9$ (note that A's shortest path to E is through C!)

   C's cost to E via D is $c(C,D) + D_D(E) = 1 + 4 = 5$

   Thus, C will route to E via D, since that path through D has minimum cost.

d.   From its neighbors, nodes B, D, and F. Note that E does not receive distance vectors from nodes A and C, since they are not direct neighbors.

e.   See page 358 in the textbook for notation.

   E's cost to B via B is $c(E,B) + D_B(B) = 10 + 0 = 10$

   E's cost to B via D is $c(E,D) + D_D(B) = 4 + 5 = 9$

   E's cost to B via F is $c(E,F) + D_F(B) = 2 + 4 = 6$

   Thus, E will route to B via F, since that path through F has minimum cost.

17. a.

	Destination					
node	A	B	C	D	E	F
A	0	5	2	3	6	8
B	5	0	3	2	1	3
C	2	3	0	1	4	6
D	3	3	1	0	3	5
E	6	1	4	3	0	2
F	8	3	6	5	2	0

   b. From its neighbors, nodes A, D, and F. Note that C does not receive distance vectors from nodes B and E, since they are not direct neighbors.

   c. See page 358 in the textbook for notation.

   C's cost to F via A is $c(C,A) + D_A(F) = 2 + 8 = 10$ (note that A's shortest path to F is through C!)
   C's cost to F via D is $c(C,D) + D_D(F) = 1 + 7 = 6$
   C's cost to F via F is $c(C,F) + D_F(F) = 18 + 0 = 18$
   Thus, C will route to F via D, since that path through D has minimum cost.

   d. From its neighbors, nodes D and E. Note that E does not receive distance vectors from nodes A, C, and F, since they are not direct neighbors.

   e. See page 358 in the textbook for notation.

   B's cost to C via D is $c(B,D) + D_D(C) = 2 + 1 = 3$
   B's cost to C via E is $c(B,E) + D_E(C) = 1 + 4 = 5$
   Thus, B will route to C via D, since that path through D has minimum cost.

18. a.

	Destination					
node	A	B	C	D	E	F
A	0	infty	2	10	infty	infty
C	2	infty	0	1	infty	18
D	10	2	1	0	11	6
F	infty	infty	18	6	2	0

b. C's distance table is unchanged. Since A's distance table does not cause C to learn of any new shorter paths to any of the destinations.

	Destination					
node	A	B	C	D	E	F
A	0	inffy	2	10	inffy	inffy
C	2	inffy	0	1	inffy	18
D	10	2	1	0	11	6
F	inffy	inffy	18	6	2	0

c.

	Destination					
node	A	B	C	D	E	F
A	0	inffy	2	10	inffy	inffy
C	2	3	0	1	12	7
D	10	2	1	0	11	6
F	inffy	inffy	18	6	2	0

19. a. A will advertise that it can reach w and y, since x needs to know which networks its provider can reach. It may also advertise that it can reach B and C. However, if B and C are only transit networks (that is, only providing service to/from their customers networks), then A would not have to advertise B and C to x.

b. X will not advertise any routes to A, since otherwise A might try to route through x, and x is a customer network, not a transit network.

c. A will advertise that it can reach w and x. Note that since C is a peer network, A will only advertise its customers to X. In particular, A wouldn't advertise y to C, since that might cause C to route to y via A.

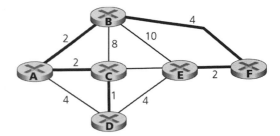

20. The following spanning trees have the same minimal cost.

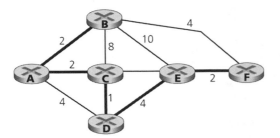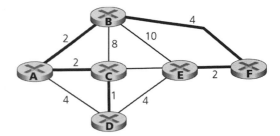

21. The set of shortest paths is:

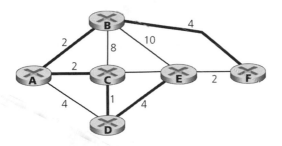

The forwarding behavior of reverse path forwarding is:

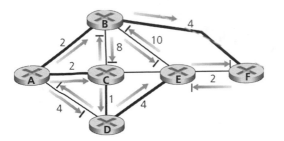

Link Layer and Local Area Networks

Most Important Ideas and Concepts from Chapter 5

♦ **Link layer services.** One of the key facets of a layered architecture is that a protocol in one layer provides services to the protocols in the layer above. In particular, a protocol in the link layer (layer 2) provides services to the protocols in the network layer (layer 3). The most basic service of any link-layer protocol is to move a datagram from one node to an adjacent node over a single communication link. As discussed on page 420 of the textbook, a useful analogy here is that of a tourist, a travel agent, transportation segments, and transportation modes (bus, plane, train, and so on). A transportation segment (say, between two cities) is analogous to a link, a transportation mode is analogous to a link-layer protocol, a tourist is analogous to a packet, and a travel agent—who plans the trip from end-to-end—is analogous to a routing protocol.

At the sender side, a link-layer protocol encapsulates the datagram in a link-layer frame, which is then passed to the physical layer for transmission over the link. At the receiving side, after receiving a frame, the link-layer protocol extracts the datagram and passes it to the network layer. Other possible services a link-layer protocol can provide include: medium access control, reliable delivery, flow control, error detection, and correction. Many of these services can also be provided in other layers. For example, we learned in Chapter 3 that the TCP transport-layer protocol provides end-to-end flow control, so that the sending side of a TCP connection does not overwhelm the receiving side of the connection. Flow-control in the link layer has a similar objective, but is no longer from end-to-end but instead from node to adjacent node. In this chapter we cover in detail many of the classic link-layer services. We also highlight many of the key services in the paragraphs below.

♦ **Error detection and correction.** Error detection is another example of a service that can be provided in different layers. The checksum in UDP and TCP are examples of an error detection service at the transport layer. Similarly, IP's header checksum is an example of error detection at the network layer. Typically, the error detection in the network and transport layers is rather crude, only detecting single-bit errors and certain combinations of multiple-bit errors. Typically more sophisticated, a link-layer error detection scheme can detect (over a single link) single bit and a wide-range of common multiple-bit errors. The main idea behind error detection is for the sender to create, as a function of the bits in the frame, a block of bits and include the block in a header field in the frame. When the receiving side of the link receives the frame, it runs the frame through the same function and compares the result with the block in the frame. If there is a match, the frame is considered error-free; if there is an inconsistency, the frame is considered corrupted. Section 5.2 discusses three error detection schemes, each scheme being more complicated and more powerful. The third scheme, cyclic redundancy check (CRC), is used in many link-layer protocols, including Ethernet and Wi-Fi. Schemes can also be designed so that not only they determine whether there is an error, but also they determine exactly which bits in the frame are in error. In this case, the receiver can simply flip the erroneous bits, thereby correcting the errors. When a scheme detects and corrects erroneous bits, it is said to provide an error correction service.

♦ **Multiple access protocols.** There are two types of network links: point-to-point links and broadcast links. A point-to-point link consists of a single sender at one end of the link and single receiver at the other end of the link; an example is a fiber-optic link between two routers. Broadcast links have multiple sending and receiving nodes, all connected to the same shared broadcast channel. For a broadcast link, when any one node transmits a frame, each of the other nodes receives a copy of the frame. Ethernet and wireless LANs (for example, Wi-Fi) are examples of broadcast links. Without any coordination among the nodes, there is the possibility that two or more nodes transmit simultaneously, causing their frames to collide at the receiving nodes. Typically, when a collision occurs, it is difficult, if not impossible, for a receiver to disentangle the colliding frames. The purpose of a multiple access protocol is to coordinate the transmissions of the senders to reduce the probability of-or even entirely eliminate-the collisions at the receivers. Three of the most desirable characteristics of a multiple access protocol for a channel of rate R follow:

(a) When M nodes have data to send, each of the M nodes gets an average throughput of R/M. Thus, the protocol is fair and makes use of all the transmission capacity, R.

(b) The protocol is decentralized.

(c) The protocol is simple.

Multiple access protocols can be classified into three categories: channel partitioning protocols, taking-turns protocols, and random access protocols. Time division multiplexing (TDM) is an excellent example of a channel partitioning protocol. To describe TDM, suppose the channel supports N nodes. TDM divides time into time frames and further divides each frame into N slots. Each slot in is then assigned to one of the N nodes. Specifically, whenever a node has a packet to send, it transmits the packet's bits during its assigned slot in the revolving TDM frame.

TDM eliminates collisions and is perfectly fair: each node gets R/N bps on average when it has something to send. But TDM has two major drawbacks. First, if only a few nodes are transmitting, then most of the channel transmission capacity is wasted. Second, when a node has something to transmit, it has to wait for its slot in the revolving frame to circle around. Token passing is the classic example of a taking turns protocol.

In token passing, a small frame, known as the token, is passed among the nodes in some fixed order, for example, from node 1 to node 2, from node 2 to node 3, and so on. A node is permitted to transmit only when it has the token. As soon as a node is finished transmitting, it passes the token to the subsequent node. Token passing is decentralized, fair, and highly efficient. However, to handle the possibility of node failures, token passing protocols are necessarily complex.

♦ **Random access protocols and ALOHA.** Random access protocols are so pervasive and important in computer networks, that they deserve a special top-ten listing for themselves. In a random access protocol, nodes independently transmit, resulting in the possibility of collisions. A node that transmits receives some feedback (to be discussed later), so that it learns whether or not its transmission was successful without a collision. If nodes have colliding frames, then these nodes retransmit their frames. Of course, if all the colliding nodes were to retransmit at the same time, there would again be collisions, making a bad situation even worse. The key idea behind a random access protocol is that after a transmitting node experiences a collision, it waits a random period of time before retransmitting. In this manner, the colliding nodes will hopefully retransmit at different times, thereby getting their frames to the receivers without collisions.

One of the simplest and well-known random access protocols is ALOHA, as described on page 435 of the textbook. In ALOHA, each node has a biased coin with the probability of a head occurring equal to p. If a node's frame collides, the node flips the coin. If the result is a head, the node retransmits the frame; otherwise the node waits a frame time and then flips the coin again. A simple probabilistic analysis shows that when there are many nodes and all nodes have many frames to transmit, the fraction of the time the channel transmits without collisions is only 37 percent. Thus, ALOHA is very inefficient when many nodes have data to send.

♦ **Link-layer addressing.** Just as human beings have many identifiers (names, social security numbers, street addresses, and so on), so do hosts in a network. We have already learned about one such identifier, namely, the host's network-layer address, which is called the IP address in the Internet. Another important identifier is the host's link-layer address or—more commonly called—the host's MAC address. The MAC address is 48 bits and is typically written in hexadecimal notation. For example, 1A-23-F9-CD-06-9B could be a MAC address for some host. Similar to a social security number, a MAC address has a flat structure, with all bits (higher- and lower-order) bits having equal importance. A MAC address does not change no matter where the host moves, again analogous to a person's social security number, which does not change even when a person changes residences. In contrast, a host's IP address is hierarchical—with a network and a host part—and does change when the host moves from one access network to another. Just as a person may find it useful to have both a postal address and a social security number, it is useful for a host to have both a network layer address and a MAC address. Routers also have multiple MAC addresses—one for each interface.

In LANs, when a node (host or router) wants to send a frame to another node in the LAN, the node inserts the destination node's MAC address into the frame. For a broadcast LAN —such as Ethernet and Wi-Fi—the frame will be received by all nodes on the LAN. Each node that receives the frame checks to see if the destination MAC address matches its own MAC address; if so, the node passes the payload of the frame to the network layer; if not, the node simply drops the frame. There is an exception to this rule, however. If the sending node uses the broadcast address (FF-FF-FF-FF-FF-FF), then all of the receiving nodes will pass the payload to their network layers.

♦ **ARP: translating between link-layer and IP addresses.** Suppose you are a host on a LAN and you want to send an IP datagram to another host on the same LAN; further suppose you know (perhaps from DNS) the destination host's IP address, but not its MAC address. Being a lazy guy and following standard practice, you give your datagram to the link layer and ask it to deliver the datagram to the destination host on your behalf. The link layer, of course, creates a link-layer frame, and inserts the IP datagram into the data field of the frame. But to deliver the frame to the destination host, the link layer must also insert the destination MAC address into the frame. So now we come to an interesting question: Knowing only the destination IP address, how is the sending host going to determine the destination MAC address? This task is the job of ARP, which stands for Address Resolution Protocol. Each node maintains an ARP table, providing the mappings from IP addresses to MAC addresses for nodes on the same LAN. Importantly, this ARP table is not configured by a network administrator. Instead, it is self-learning, that is, it learns about the mappings as it needs them. Specifically, if a sending node needs to translate an IP address to a MAC address, and the mapping is currently not in the table, the sending node sends an ARP query message, as part of a broadcast frame, into the LAN. The destination node—which of course knows its own MAC and IP addresses—answers with an ARP response message, providing the desired mapping.

ARP is localized to a subnet—in particular a host does not use ARP to determine the MAC address of a host on a different subnet. Instead, the host uses ARP to determine the MAC address of the router that is in the same subnet and that is along the path to the destination host. When the frame arrives at the router, the router extracts the IP datagram and then inserts the datagram in a new link-layer frame for forwarding to the next node (either another router or the destination host).

♦ **Ethernet.** Ethernet is an immensely popular LAN technology. The Ethernet frame itself provides significant insight into Ethernet and link-layer protocols in general, and should be memorized. It has exactly six fields: a preamble field used by the receiving host to synchronize its clock to the sending clock and to determine when the frame begins; source and destination MAC address fields; a data field, which carries the IP datagram; a CRC field for error checking; and a type field, which indicates the type of payload (IP datagram, ARP packet, and so on). Ethernet uses the CSMA/CD protocol, which is a random access protocol along the lines of unslotted ALOHA, but with some features that exploit the local area setting. In particular, in CSMA/CD, when a host knows that another host is transmitting, it refrains, thereby averting a collision; and when a host starts to transmit but learns shortly afterwards that another host has just started to transmit, it aborts its transmission and begins a random access procedure. Ethernet has many seen many technological variations over the years, starting at 10 Mbps and moving up to 10

Gbps. However, the Ethernet frame structure and CSMA/CD access have always been part of Ethernet. In the not-so-distant past, Ethernet used a bus topology. However, today Ethernet nodes are connected in a star topology.

♦ **LAN interconnection.** LANs can be interconnected with hubs, bridges, or switches. Hubs are a physical-layer interconnection device and simply repeat bits coming from a link to all other links connected to the hub. Switches are link-layer interconnection devices, processing link-layer frames. Routers, as we saw in Chapter 4, are network-layer devices, acting on link-layer and network-layer header fields. Let's give some special attention to switches, as they illustrate some new networking concepts. Like routers, switches can forward a packet to the appropriate outbound link. This is done with the aid of a switch table, in which an entry is a mapping from a destination MAC address to a switch interface. As you recall from Chapter 4, the entries in a router's forwarding table are either configured manually or are configured via a routing protocol, such as OSPF. The entries in a switching table are acquired through a *self-learning mechanism:* when a frame arrives on one of its interfaces, the switch examines the frame's source MAC address and creates an entry for that MAC address in its table. Entries that are not refreshed with new packets are purged from the table after a (typically configurable) timeout period. Finally, if a frame arrives to the switch and there isn't an entry for the frame's destination address, the frame is broadcast into all the other links connected to the switch.

♦ **Link-layer protocols for a point-to-point link.** There are two types of links: broadcast links and point-to-point links. Protocols for point-to-point links are naturally simpler and more straightforward. Section 5.7 examines the issues surrounding point-to-point protocols using a specific illustrative example, namely, the Point-to-Point Protocol (PPP), which is the protocol of choice for a dial-up link for residential access. PPP provides packet framing, transparency (that is, it doesn't place constraints on the bits that are carried in PPP's payload), network-layer protocol independence, link-type independence, error detection, connection liveliness, and network-layer address negotiation. To achieve transparency, PPP uses byte-stuffing, which is used to distinguish control flag bit patterns with identical data bit patterns. Byte-stuffing is an important networking concept that appears in many protocols in many layers.

♦ **Asynchronous Transfer Mode: link virtualization.** ATM provides an alternative suite of protocols to the TCP/IP protocol suite. The original designers of ATM had hoped that global networks would be built with the ATM protocol suite; but much to their chagrin, the Internet and TCP/IP became dominant and pervasive, leaving little room for ATM. However, ATM merits discussion for two reasons. First, it provides an alternative protocol suite—with an alternative service model—to TCP/IP. Second, it is actually deployed at the link layer, as we discuss in Section 5.8.

Review Questions

This section provides additional study questions. Answers to each question are provided in the next section.

1. **Two-dimensional parity scheme.** Suppose the information content of a packet is the bit pattern 1110101010101111 and an even parity scheme is being used. What would the value of the checksum field be for the case of a two-dimensional parity scheme? Your answer should be such that a minimum-length checksum field is used.

2. **Cyclic Redundancy Check (CRC).** Consider the 4-bit generator $G = 1001$, and suppose that D has the value 111010. What is the value of R?

3. **Efficiency of slotted ALOHA.** Section 5.3 outlines a derivation of the efficiency of slotted ALOHA. In this problem, we will examine a special case. Suppose there are exactly three nodes, all with an infinite number of packets to transmit. Let p be the probability that a node transmits in any slot.

    a. As a function of p, find the probability that there is a successful transmission in any given slot.

    b. Find the value of p that maximizes this expression.

    c. What is the maximum efficiency for $N = 3$?

4. **Polling.** Consider a broadcast channel with N nodes and a transmission rate of R bps. Suppose the broadcast channel uses polling (with an additional polling node) for its multiple access. Suppose the amount of time from when a node completes transmission until the subsequent node is permitted to transmit (that is, the polling delay) is t_{poll}. Suppose that within a polling round, a given node is allowed to transmit at most Q bits. Further suppose node 1, initially with no bits to send, receives Q bits to send. What is the maximum time from when node 1 receives the bits until it can begin to send them?

5. **CSMA/CD.** In CSMA/CD, after the fourth collision, what is the probability that the node chooses $K = 3$? The result $K = 3$ corresponds to a delay of how many microseconds on a 10 Mbps Ethernet?

6. **Carrier sense and collision detection.** Suppose nodes A and B are on the same 10 Mbps Ethernet segment, and the propagation delay between the two nodes is 225 bit times. Suppose at time $t = 0$, B starts to transmit a frame. Suppose A also transmits at some $t = x$, but before completing its transmission it receives bits from B (hence, a collision occurs at A). Assuming node A follows the CSMA/CD protocol, what is the maximum value of x?

7. **Carrier sense and collision detection.** Consider two nodes A and B on the same Ethernet segment, and suppose the propagation delay between the two nodes is 225 bit times. Suppose at time t = 0, both nodes A and B begin to transmit a frame. At what time do they detect the collision? Assuming both nodes transmit a 48-bit jam signal after detecting a collision, at what time (in bit times) do nodes A and B sense an idle channel? How many seconds is this for a 10 Mbps Ethernet?

8. **Ethernet efficiency.** Consider a 100 Mbps 100BaseT Ethernet. Suppose the maximum propagation delay between any two nodes on the Ethernet is .512 microseconds. What is the efficiency of this LAN? Assume a frame length of 64 bytes and that there are no repeaters.

9. **Link-layer services and Ethernet.** Section 5.1.1 lists a number of different services that a link layer can potentially provide to the network layer. These services include: a) framing, b) medium access, c) reliable delivery, d) flow control, e) error detection, f) error correction, g) full-duplex and half-duplex. For each of these services, discuss how or how not Ethernet provides the service.

10. **Ethernet broadcast packets.** List two protocols that require Ethernet to use broadcast frames. Explain.

11. **ARP delays.** Consider transmitting a packet from host A to host B via a router, as shown below:

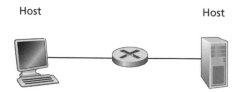

Suppose that before sending the packet, all the ARP tables (in the two hosts and in the router) are empty. Let x denote the time to transmit a packet. Let y denote the delay from beginning the transmission of an ARP query until receiving and processing an ARP response. Ignore propagation delays. Assuming host A knows the IP address of host B, what is the total delay in moving the packet from Host A to Host B?

12. **Self-learning switch.** Consider an Ethernet LAN consisting of N nodes interconnected with a switch. Suppose the switch's forwarding table is initially empty. Suppose node A wants to TCP three-way handshake with node B, where both nodes are on the LAN. Assuming this is the only traffic on the network, and there are no packet errors or loss, how many frames will be transmitted in the process of establishing the TCP connection? Assume node A knows the IP address of node B, and ARP tables have all the necessary mappings.

13. **Self-learning switch and ARP.** Repeat the above problem, but now assume that the ARP tables are also initially empty.

14. **Self-learning switch, ARP, and DNS.** Repeat the above problem, but now also suppose that Host A only knows the hostname of Host B (and not its IP address). Assume the DNS server is Host C in the LAN, and Host A knows the IP address of the DNS server.

15. **Addressing at the network and link layers, routing versus switching.** (This question concerns material from Chapters 4 and 5.) Consider the network shown below. Each of the subnets A-D contains at most 31 hosts; subnet E connects routers R1 and R2.

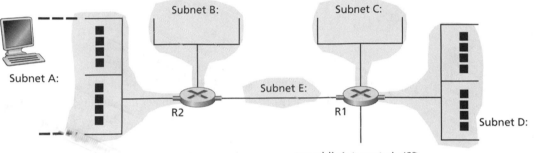

a. Assign network addresses to the five subnets shown above (that is, write down the addresses you have assigned)

b. Assign (write down) a full (32-bit) IP address for each the two hosts shown in subnets A and D.

c. Assign (write down) a full IP address to the router interface in subnet E.

d. What is the network prefix advertised by router R1 to the public Internet?

e. Assign (write down) a MAC address to D.

f. Does the host in A ever need to know the MAC address of the R1's interface in subnet E in order to send an IP packet to the host in D? Explain your answer in one or two sentences.

Now suppose that router R2 above is replaced by an Ethernet *switch*, S2 (Router R1 remains a router).

g. Are the interfaces that previously were in subnets A, B, and E still in the same separate three IP subnets now that R2 is replaced by S2? Explain your answer in a few sentences.

h. In order to send an IP packet to the host in D, does the host in A ever need to know the MAC address of the R1's left interface now that R2 is

replaced by S2? If so, how does it get the MAC address of R1's left interface? Explain your answer in one or two sentences.

16. **Addressing at the network and link layers, routing versus switching.**

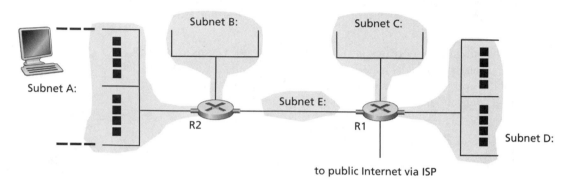

(This question concerns material from Chapters 4 and 5.)

Consider the network shown above Each of the subnets A-D contains at most

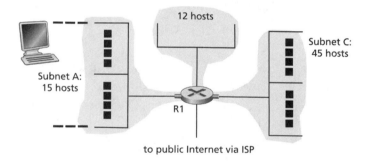

31 hosts; subnet E connects routers R1 and R2.

a. Consider the network shown above, consisting of a single router, R1,
with three subnets A, B and C, with 15, 12, and 45 hosts respectively on
these subnets. Assign an address range to the hosts in subnets A, B, and
C such that only a single aggregated address need be advertised by R1 to
the public Internet, and that the size of the aggregated address ranges that
is advertised is minimized. In a sentence or two, explain how you arrived
at your answer.

b. Assign a specific Internet address and MAC address to the host shown in
subnet A, an Internet address and MAC address to the host shown in subnet C, and a MAC address and IP address to each router interface. These
addresses (both Internet and MAC) can be of your own choosing. Consider an IP datagram sent from the host in Subnet A that is destined to the

host in subnet C. This IP datagram is contained in an Ethernet frame sent from the host in subnet C to router R1. What are the source and destination MAC addresses of this Ethernet frame? What are the source and destination address in the IP datagram contained in this Ethernet frame?

c. Now consider the Ethernet frame carrying this IP datagram from the router to the host in subnet C. What are the source and destination MAC addresses of this Ethernet frame? What are the source and destination addresses in the IP datagram contained in this Ethernet frame?

17. **Multiple access protocols: voice-over-IP and data.** In this chapter, we studied a number of multiple access protocols, including TDMA, CSMA, slotted Aloha, and token passing.

a. Suppose you were charged with putting together a large LAN to support IP telephony (only) and that multiple users may want to carry on a phone call at the same time. Recall that IP telephony digitizes and packetizes voice at a constant bit rate when a user is making an IP phone call. How well suited are these four protocols for this scenario? Provide a brief (one sentence) explanation of each answer.

b. Now suppose you were charged with putting together a LAN to support the occasional exchange of data between nodes (in this part of this question, there is no voice traffic). That is, any individual node does not have data to send very often. How well suited are these four protocols for this scenario? Provide a brief (one sentence) explanation of each answer.

c. Now suppose the LAN must support both voice and data and you must choose one of these multiple access strategies in order to support both applications on the same network, with the understanding that voice calls are more important than data. Which would you choose and why? How would voice and data be sent in this scenario? That is, which access protocol would you use, or adapt/modify, and why?

Answers to Review Questions

1. The minimum-length checksum is obtained by arranging the 16 bits in four rows and four columns. We then add an additional row and column for the parity bits. Below, the rightmost column and bottom row are for parity bits:

    11101
    10100
    10100
    11110
    00011

2. R is the remainder of $D \cdot 2^r/G$, where $r = 3$ since G has 4 bits. Thus, we divide 1001 into 111010000 to get 111101 with remainder $R = 101$. So we send (data + CRC) 111010101. To check this result we multiply G times 111101, which gives $= 111010101$. To this we add R, which gives 111010000, which is exactly equal to $2^r D$.

3. a. Consider one of the nodes. It has a success if and only if it transmits and the other two nodes do not transmit. The probability that it transmits is p; the probability that the second node does not transmit is $(1 - p)$; and the probability that the third node doesn't transmit is $(1 - p)$. Since each of these events are independent, the probability that only the first node transmits is $p(1 - p)(1 - p) = p(1 - p)^2$. Now, a success occurs if any of three nodes have a success. Thus the overall probability of success is probability that the first node has a success plus the probability the second node has a success plus the probability that the third node has a success, which is $3p(1 - p)^2$.

    b. To find the p that maximizes the probability of success, we differentiate $f(p) = p(1 - p)^2$, set the result to zero, and solve for p. The derivative of $f(p)$ is $f(p) = (1 - p)^2 + 2p(1 - p) = (3p - 1)(p - 1)$. The value $p = 1$ minimizes the probability; the value $p = 1/3$ maximizes the probability.

    c. With $p = 1/3$, the probability of success (equivalently, the efficiency) is $3(1/3)(1 - 1/3)^2 = 4/9$.

4. Node 1 must wait to be polled. In the worst case, all other nodes have Q bits to send, and the Q bits arrive to node 1 just after node 1 completes a transmission. Before node 1 gets polled again, $N - 1$ other nodes transmit Q bits at rate R, giving a delay of $(N - 1)Q/R$. In addition to this, there are N polling delays. So the total wait is $(N - 1)Q/R + N t_{poll}$.

5. The node chooses K from the elements in the set $\{0, 1, 2, \dots, 15\}$ with equal probability. The probability that it chooses $K = 3$ is thus 1/16. With $K = 3$,

the node waits $3 \cdot 512 = 1{,}536$ bit times. The corresponding delay over a 10 Mbps Ethernet link is $(1536 \text{ bits})/(10^7 \text{ bits/sec}) = 153.6$ microseconds.

6. Node A senses an empty channel from time $t = 0$ to time $t = 225$. Node A can transmit at any time in this interval. At time $t = 225$, Node A senses a busy channel and will refrain from transmitting. So the maximum value of x is $x = 224$.

7. Both nodes A and B detect the collision at time $t = 225$. At time $t = 225 + 48 = 273$ both nodes stop transmitting their jam signals. The last bit of the jam signal from B arrives at A at time $t = 273 + 225 = 498$ bit times. Similarly, the last bit of the jam signal from B arrives at A at time $t = 273 + 225 = 498$ bit times. For a 10 Mbps Ethernet, this corresponds to $(498 \text{ bits})/(10^7 \text{ bits/sec}) = 49.8$ microseconds.

8. The efficiency is $1/(1 + 5a)$ where $a = t_{prop}/t_{trans}$. We have $t_{prop} = .512$ microseconds and $t_{trans} = (512 \text{ bits})/(10^8 \text{ bits/sec}) = 5.12$ microseconds. Thus, the efficiency is $1/(1 + 5/10) = .6667$.

9. a. Framing: Ethernet encapsulates the payload (such as an IP datagram) in an Ethernet frame. Included in this encapsulation is the preamble, which helps the receiving node determine where the frame begins and helps the receiving node synchronize its clock to the frame.

   b. Ethernet provides CSMA/CD medium access.

   c. Reliable delivery: Ethernet does not provide reliable delivery. Receivers do not send ACKS or NACKS to senders; senders do not maintain timers for transmitted frames. Thus, if a receiver determines that a frame has errors, it simply discards the frame. Higher-layer protocols may eventually retransmit the frame.

   d. Ethernet does not provide flow control. Thus, if the network layer in the receiving node does not read data out of the adapter fast enough, the sender can overflow the link-layer receive buffer in the adapter.

   e. Ethernet does perform error-detection using the CRC field in the Ethernet frame. If an error is detected, it discards the frame.

   f. Ethernet does not correct bit errors.

   g. Generally, CSMA/CD is half-duplex, as packets collide if transmitted at the same time. However, if all nodes are connected through a full-duplex switch, then Ethernet is full-duplex.

10. ARP: An ARP query is encapsulated in an Ethernet broadcast frame; however, the response is sent in a unicast frame. DHCP: The DHCP discover message is also sent within an Ethernet broadcast frame (after encapsulation in an IP broadcast datagram!).

11. First Host A does an ARP query-response exchange with the router, taking y. Then it sends the packet to the router, taking x. The router does an ARP query-response exchange with Host B, taking y. Then it sends the packet to Host B, taking y. So the total time is 2y + 2x.

12. Node A creates a TCP SYN packet, which (after encapsulation in an IP datagram) gets encapsulated into an Ethernet frame. This Ethernet frame will have B's MAC address for its destination address. Node A transmits the frame. When the frame arrives at the switch, the switch will take note of A's location and then transmit the frame onto the other N − 1 links, giving a total of N transmissions so far. When B receives the frame, it will send a SYNACK, encapsulated in an Ethernet frame with A's MAC address for the destination address. Thus, there are N + 1 frames so far. When the switch receives the frame, it will take note of B's location; it will already have an entry in its table for A and thus will only transmit the frame onto one link. Thus, there are N + 2 frames so far. When A receives the SYNACK it will send an ACK. Two more transmissions are required for this ACK, giving a total of N + 4 transmitted frames.

13. Because the ARP tables are empty, first host A must send out an ARP query within an Ethernet broadcast frame. This will generate 1 transmission at A and N − 1 transmissions at the switch. Then host B will respond with an ARP response, which will generate 2 transmissions, giving a total of N + 2 so far. In this process, host B will update its ARP table with an entry for host A. Also, during this ARP exchange, the switch will learn about the locations of hosts A and B. Thus, when host A sends a SYN, the switch can send the SYN packet directly to B. The TCP handshake will therefore generate an additional 6 Ethernet frames, giving a total of N + 8 frames.

14. First Host A needs to do an ARP exchange with node C to get node C's MAC address. This generates N + 2 Ethernet frames. This also generates entries for A and C in the switch table. Then node A must do a DNS exchange with C. This will generate 4 Ethernet frames, giving N + 6 frames thus far. Node A will now have B's IP address, but not B's MAC address. So A will have to do an ARP exchange with B. Since B is not yet in the switch table, the ARP exchange will generate another N + 2 Ethernet frames, giving a total of 2N + 8 frames thus far. The TCP exchange will then generate another 6 frames, giving a total of 2N + 14 frames.

15. a. Each subnet needs to address up to 31 hosts, using the rightmost 5 bits of the address. The five subnet addresses are thus x.y.z.000_/27, x.y.z.001_/27, x.y.z.010_/27, x.y.z.011_/27, x.y.z.100_/27, where the notation x.y.z.000_ means that the leftmost three bits of the fourth address byte are 000. Other answers with different bit values in bits 25, 26, 27 are also possible, as long as the five three-bit patterns used are unique.

   b. If you chose an address range x.y.z.000_/27 for network A, then the address you choose here must have these 27 leading bits, and can have any

5 remaining bits you want. If you chose an address range x.y.z.011_/27 for network D, then the address you choose here must have these 27 leading bits, and can have any 5 remaining bits you want.

c. If you chose an address range x.y.z.100_/27 for network E, then the address you choose here must have these 27 leading bits, and can have any 5 remaining bits you want.

d. x.y.x./24

e. Any 48 bit number is OK.

f. No. The host in subnet A needs to address a link-layer frame (containing the IP packet addresses to the host in D) to the R2 interface in subnet A only.

g. No. They are now all in the same subnet from an IP addressing point of view, since there is no longer any intervening router.

h. Yes. Now the host in A now needs to address its link-layer frame to the left interface of R1. The host in A gets the MAC address of the left interface of R1 using ARP. The host in A knows that in order to route its packet to the host in D, it must first send that packet (over Ethernet) to router R1, whose IP address is in the hosts routing table. Thus, it uses ARP to get the MAC address associated with the IP address of R1's left interface.

16. a. Given the stated number of hosts, subnet A requires at least 4 bits of addressing, subnet B requires at least 4 bits of addressing, and subnet C requires at least 6 bits of addressing. Let the first 3 bytes of the address for all of the hosts be X.Y.Z.

   • The address for hosts in subnet C is in the range X.Y.Z.00_, where the last byte of the address begins with two zeros and the rest of the 6 bits are used to address hosts in C. Note that the second bit in the last byte is a 0. For subsets A and B, this bit will be a 1.

   • The address for hosts in subnet B is in the range X.Y.Z.010_. The last byte of the address begins with 010 and the final 5 bits can be used to address the hosts in B.

   • The address for hosts in subnet A is in the range X.Y.Z.011_. The last byte of the address begins with 011 (which differs from the leading 010 for subnet B, and the leading 00 for subnet C) and the final 5 bits can be used to address the hosts in A.

   The size of the single aggregated network that is advertised is thus X.Y.Z.0/25-the last seven bits are used to address hosts in subnets A, B, and C.

   b. • Let the host in A have IP address 128.119.40.011000001 (where we have abused notation and shown the last byte in binary format) and MAC address aa:aa:aa:aa:aa:aa.

- Let the router interface into subnet A have IP address 128.119.40.01100010, and MAC address bb:bb:bb:bb:bb:bb.
- Let the host in C have IP address 128.119.40.000000001 (where we have abused notation and shown the last byte in binary format) and MAC address cc:cc:cc:cc:cc:cc:cc.
- Let the router interface into subnet C have IP address 128.119.40.00000010, and MAC address dd:dd:dd:dd:dd:dd:dd.

The IP datagram from the host in subset A to the router interface in subnet A has IP source 128.119.40.011000001 and IP destination 128.119.40.000000001. The source MAC address is aa:aa:aa:aa:aa:aa, and the destination MAC address is bb:bb:bb:bb:bb:bb.

c. The IP datagram from the router interface in subnet C to the destination host in subnet C has IP source 128.119.40.011000001 and IP destination 128.119.40.000000001-the same answer as in (b). The source MAC address is cc:cc:cc:cc:cc:cc:cc, and the destination MAC address is dd:dd:dd:dd:dd:dd:dd.

17. a. TDMA works well here since it provides a constant bit rate service of 1 slot per frame. CSMA will not work as work well here (unless the channel utilization is low) due to collisions and variable amount of time needed to access the channel (for example, channel access delays can be unbounded) and the need for voice packets to be played out synchronously and with low delay at the receiver. Slotted Aloha has the same answer as CSMA. Token passing works well here since each station gets a turn to transmit once per token round, yielding an essentially constant bit rate service.

b. TDMA would not work well here as if there is only one station with something to send, it can only send once per frame. Hence, the access delays are long (one half frame time on average), and the throughput over a long period of time is only 1/N of the channel capacity. CSMA would work well since at low utilization, a node will get to use the channel as soon as it need to. Slotted Aloha has the same answer as CSMA Token passing would work better than TDMA but slightly less well than CSMA and Slotted Aloha, since it must wait for the token to be passed to the other stations (who likely wouldn't use it) before sending again.

c. Here are two possible answers. One approach would be to divide the channel into two "pieces"-one for data packets and one for voice. This can be accomplished by assigning some number of TDMA slots for voice calls (for example, one slot to each user). Also, add some additional slots and allow the stations with data to send to perform random access (for example, slotted aloha or CSMA) within those data slots only. A second approach would be to use token passing with priorities, and give priority to voice packets.

Wireless and Mobile Networks

Most Important Ideas and Concepts from Chapter 6

♦ **Wireless and mobility: each poses very different challenges.** In this chapter, we drew an important distinction between *communication over a wireless link*, and the *mobility* that wireless links enable. These topics, which roughly comprise the first and second half of the chapter, pose very different challenges. Communication over a wireless link is, as the name implies, primarily a link layer (that is, a single hop) problem. Wireless link communication protocols send link-layer frames between a sender and a receiver(s) over a single hop, in much the same way as the wired LAN protocols (for example, Ethernet) that we studied in Chapter 5. However, wireless communication protocols must deal with the more difficult characteristics of the wireless link—the hidden terminal problem, and link errors resulting from interference, fading, and multipath (see "How a wireless broadcast link differs from a wired broadcast link" below).

Mobility—the challenge of communicating with a host that changes its point of attachment to the network—is made possible by wireless links. But as shown in Figure 6.16 on page 536 of the textbook, mobility is also possible in wired networks. For example, a host can change its point of attachment to the network from one wired location to another wired location. Many discussions of wireless and mobility treat the two topics as inextricably intertwined. Here, we'll consider the problems posed by each separately.

♦ **Wireless networks: infrastructure mode versus ad hoc.** In Section 6.1, we learned that there are two types of wireless networks: those that operate in *infrastructure mode*, and those that operate in *ad hoc mode*. We encounter infrastructure-mode networks in our daily lives, for example, when we attach our wireless device to an 802.11 wireless access point in an Internet café or classroom. In infrastructure mode networks, an access point (a.k.a. base station) is present, and typically connected directly to the wired network (see Figure 6.1 on page 506 of the textbook). When a wireless host first enters an infrastructure network (for example, when you sit down in the café or classroom, and power up your laptop), it must first *associate* with the access point (see pages 515–516 of the textbook). All communication to and from the wireless host is then over the wireless channel between the host and the base station. Indeed, two wireless hosts in the same wireless infrastructure network (for example, two café patrons, or two of the wireless hosts in the upper-left circle shown in Figure 6.1) will communicate with each other via the base station. Note the important role of the base station—it connects the wireless host to the rest of the network, where services such as network-layer address assignment (typically via DHCP) and routing are performed, in much the same way that a wired Ethernet switch (Section 5.6.2) connects a wired host to the rest of the network.

In an ad hoc network, no base station is present. An ad hoc network might be formed for example, when users are in proximity of each other on a train, or better yet on a remote island beach, where no infrastructure is present. Consequently, the individual hosts themselves must perform functions such as address-assignment and routing (when the hosts in the wireless ad hoc network are connected via multiple wireless hops). Currently, ad hoc networking is an area of active research, and thus is a topic beyond the scope of our introductory text.

♦ **Code Division Multiple Access (CDMA).** In Chapter 5, we learned that hosts can share a broadcast channel in either frequency (for example, FDMA) or in time (for example, TDMA). In Sections 5.3.2 and 5.3.3, we studied various random access protocols that share the channel in time. CDMA provides yet another way for multiple users to share a broadcast channel. In CDMA, each user has a different M-bit code. Each original data bit to be sent by the user is first multiplied by each of the M bits in the code, producing a sequence of M bits (that is, each original bit is transformed into M bits via this multiplication) that are sent into the channel. The properties of the codes are such that when two or more users send their M bits simultaneously, a receiver knowing a given sender's code can extract the sender's original data bit out of the additively-interfering bits sent by the multiple users. Recall that simultaneous transmissions by two or more users in the time-sharing random access protocols that we studied in Chapter 5 result in interference, with no message being received successfully. In CDMA, two users can send simultaneously and a receiver can still extract the message from one of the senders. Indeed, two different receivers can extract two different messages sent by two different "interfering" CDMA senders if the receivers each have the codes of the different senders (see review Questions 2 and 3 on pages 98 and 99).

♦ **How a wireless broadcast link differs from a wired broadcast link.** The physical characteristics of a wireless link are significantly different from those of a wired link, with these differences resulting in wireless multiple access protocols that are significantly different from their wired counterparts. First, *signal attenuation*—the decrease in a signal's strength as it propagates—is much more significant in a wireless network than in a wired network. In a wired network, all hosts connected to the broadcast medium (for example, the same Ethernet segment) can "hear" each other. In a wireless network, signal fading results in scenarios such as that shown in Figure 6.3(b) in the textbook, where host B can hear both hosts A and C, but hosts A and C cannot hear each other. As a result, A cannot hear a transmission from C to B, and may thus transmit a frame to B that collides with an ongoing frame transmission from C to B. A second difference between wireless and wired networks is that physical objects may block or degrade wireless signals, again resulting in a situation in which not all wireless hosts can hear the transmissions of the other wireless hosts (for example, see Figure 6.3(a) in the textbook). Finally, a third difference is that bit errors are more likely in a wireless link than in a wired link, as a result of electromagnetic interference and multipath propagation.

♦ **CSMA/CA and the RTS/CTS mechanism.** The CSMA/CA protocol and the RTS/CTS mechanism are part of the IEEE 802.11 specification. With more than

100 million Wi-Fi chipsets sold per year, 802.11 is arguably the most important wireless network access protocol, and thus a good topic for our top-10 list here! Since the details of the CSMA/CA and RTS/CTS protocols are provided in the text, we won't repeat them here, but instead provide some context and insight into the mechanisms. Similar to the other CSMA protocols we studied in Chapter 5, CSMA/CA senses the channel and will only transmit when the channel is sensed idle. Unlike CSMA/CD, however, CSMA/CA does *not* detect collisions and thus *cannot* abort transmissions when a collision occurs. Instead, frames are transmitted in their entirety—making a collision an expensive event, since the channel will be wasted for the entire duration of the frame's transmission. CSMA/CA has several features that cope with the challenges caused by signal attenuation and the hidden terminal problem shown in Figure 6.9 on page 521 of the textbook. First, CSMA/CA has an explicit ACK mechanism, allowing the sender to know that a frame has been received successfully. Recall from our discussion above and in the text that a node cannot necessarily "hear" whether its transmission was successfully received at the destination due to attenuation and the hidden terminal problem. A second important feature of 802.11 is the RTS/CTS mechanism, which allows a station to reserve the channel for a data message and its subsequent ACK. When RTS/CTS is used, collisions among RTS/CTS messages (rather than data frames) can still occur, but since the RTS/CTS messages are smaller than data frames, the overhead incurred by a collision is less.

♦ **Direct versus indirect routing to a mobile host.** In Chapter 6, we identified two basic approaches by which a correspondent can send data to a mobile host—the *indirect* approach and the *direct* approach. An *indirect approach* is taken by both mobile IP (for routing datagrams to a mobile IP host) and GSM (for routing a phone call to a mobile telephone user). In the indirect approach, the correspondent sends all traffic (IP datagrams in the case of mobile IP, or the telephone call, in the case of GSM) to the mobile host's home network. The home network knows the foreign network where the mobile host is located (see "Home and foreign agents" in the next bulleted entry). The home network then relays the data that it receives from the correspondent to the foreign network where the mobile host is located. The indirect approach works by adding a level of indirection—the home agent—between the sender and the receiver. This use of indirection is another example of the aphorism attributed variously to Butler Lampson and David Wheeler: "All problems in computer science can be solved by another level of indirection."

In the *direct approach*, a correspondent sends its traffic (IP datagrams in the case of mobile IP, or the telephone call in the case of GSM) directly to the mobile host in the foreign network. Of course, first the correspondent must determine the address of the mobile host in the foreign network, and must be notified if the mobile host moves from one foreign network to another. This requires that the correspondent knows whether the mobile is in its home network; it also requires that the correspondent use a different protocol to communicate with the destination host depending on whether or not the destination host is in its home network. Recall that in the indirect approach, the correspondent doesn't need to know whether the destination host is in its home network or visiting a foreign network—that is, the mobility of the destination host is *transparent* to the correspondent. This transparency tremendously simplifies the correspondent's task in communicating with a potentially mobile host. Indeed, the correspondent's actions are exactly the same in both scenarios.

♦ **Home and foreign agents.** The home agent and foreign agent are software processes that execute in the mobile host's home and foreign network, respectively. They interact with each other to play a crucial role in supporting a host's mobility. In our discussion here, we'll assume that an indirect approach is taken (see "Direct versus indirect routing to a mobile host" above). The *home agent's* role is two-fold. First, it keeps track of the foreign network in which the mobile host is located. This is done via a foreign-agent-to-home-agent registration protocol (see page 543 of the textbook) in which a foreign agent notifies the home agent when the mobile host joins the foreign agent's network. The second job of the home agent is to relay incoming traffic (IP datagrams in the case of mobile IP, or the telephone call in the case of GSM) received from a correspondent to the mobile host (Step 2 in Figure 6.18 in the textbook). The foreign agent is a process running in the foreign network; it too has two principal roles. First, it forwards traffic that that has been relayed by the home agent to the mobile host (Step 3 in Figure 6.18). Its second job is to let the mobile host's home agent know when the mobile host joins its (the foreign agent's) network.

♦ **Handoffs.** A *handoff* occurs when a mobile host moves from one foreign network to another—that is, changes its point of attachment to the network. If the mobile host is receiving relayed data when it moves between foreign networks, then this relayed data must be re-directed to the foreign network to which the mobile host is newly attached (see Review Question 10 on pages 102–103). In mobile IP, redirection occurs when the foreign agent in the new network notifies the home agent in the mobile host's home network that the mobile host has newly joined its (the foreign agent's) network. The home agent then redirects incoming datagrams to the new foreign agent, who relays the datagrams to the mobile host. In GSM cellular telephony, the redirection point is not in the home network, but rather in the mobile switching center (MSC) that is responsible for routing calls to the foreign network; this MSC is typically "close" to the foreign network. Figure 6.26 on page 555 of the textbook shows the steps involved in a handoff when the old base station and the new base station to which the mobile host is attaching are controlled by the same MSC. When the old base station and the new base station are controlled by different MSCs, an inter-MSC handoff is required, making the handoff is a bit more complex. Inter-MCS handoff is shown in Figure 6.27 on page 556 of the textbook.

♦ **Mobile IP.** Mobile IP is a proposed Internet Standard protocol (see RFC 3344 for Mobile IPv4 and RFC 3775 for Mobile IPv6); our discussion below involves Mobile IPv4. Mobile IPv4 takes an indirect routing approach (see "Direct versus indirect routing to a mobile host" above), and a home agent and a foreign agent, as described above. The mobile host has a home address, that is, "a long-term IP address on a home network" [RFC 3344], and a care-of-address in the foreign network being visited. As discussed above (and in detail in the textbook), the role of the home agent is to relay incoming datagrams that are initially delivered to the mobile host's home network, to the mobile node in the foreign network. This is accomplished via *tunneling*—a process in which the home agent takes the initial datagram from the correspondent and encapsulates it within another IP datagram and then addresses and sends this latter datagram to the mobile host's care-of-address in the foreign network. A useful analogy here is the mobile twenty-something-year-old who has moved out of her parent's home. Friends may still send her letters at her parent's address. (Of course, realistically, few if any twenty-something-year-olds write letters these days, preferring e-mail, IM, and SMS. But let's assume for pedagogical purposes, that twenty-something-year-olds still write letters). Suppose that a friend has sent a letter to our mobile twenty-something-year-old at her parents' address. A parent (the home agent in IP parlance) takes such a letter (the IP datagram), unopened, places (encapsulates) it in a larger envelope (another IP datagram), and then addresses the larger envelope to the twenty-something-year-old's new address (care-of-address). The postal service (IP network) then delivers the envelope (IP datagram) to the person's current address (care-of-address).

♦ **Mobility, wireless, and upper layer protocols.** The challenges posed by wireless links and mobile hosts are not confined to the link and networks layers, even though in the textbook our focus is on these lower layers. A packet that is lost on a noisy wireless link will be interpreted by TCP as a congestion-induced loss, and will result in a decrease in TCP's sending rate even though the end-to-end path may well be congestion-free. Handoff delays may result in long packet delivery delays and loss, causing glitches in the audio and video playout. Of course, many exciting applications are enabled by mobility, particularly location-aware applications.

Review Questions

This section provides additional study questions. Answers to each question are provided in the next section.

1. **The performance consequences of channel fading in multi-hop wireless networks.**

    a. Consider the scenario shown below, in which there are four wireless nodes, A, B, C, and D. The radio coverage of the four nodes is shown via the shaded ovals; all nodes share the same frequency. When A transmits, it can only be heard/received by B; when B transmits, both A and C can hear/receive from B; when C transmits both B and D (but not A) can hear/receive from C; when D transmits, only C can hear/receive from D. Now suppose that node A has an infinite supply of messages that it wants to send to D; there are no other messages in the network. A message from A must first be sent to B, which then sends the message to C, which turn sends the message to D. Time is slotted, with a message transmission time taking exactly one time slot, for example, as in slotted Aloha. During a slot, a node can do one of the following: (*i*) send a message (if it has a message to be forward toward D); (*ii*) receive a message (if exactly one is being sent to it), (*iii*) remain silent. As always, if a node hears two or more simultaneous transmissions, a collision occurs and none of the transmitted messages are received successfully. You can assume that there are no bit level errors, and thus, if exactly one message is sent, it will be received correctly by those within the transmission radius of the sender.

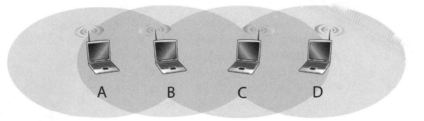

    Now suppose that an omniscient controller (that is, a controller that knows the state of every node in the network) can command each node to do whatever it (the omniscient controller) wishes, that is, to send a message, to receive a message, or to remain silent. Given this omniscient controller, what is the maximum rate at which messages can be transferred from A to D?

b. Now suppose that the wireless links in the figure above are replaced by wired links. Again, a node can send exactly one message per time slot over a link, but now a node can send a message while it is receiving a message, and simultaneous transmission over two different links do not interfere. In this wired scenario, what is the maximum rate at which messages can be transferred from A to D?

c. Now suppose we are again in the wireless scenario, and that for every data message going from A to D, D will send an ACK message that must be forwarded back to A. What is the maximum rate at which data messages can be transferred from A to D?

2. **A multi-sender CDMA example.** In this example, we consider a CDMA scenario with two senders and two receivers. The chipping rate is 8 mini-slots for each data bit, that is, $M = 8$, as shown in Figure 6.4 in the textbook. The 8-bit CDMA code for sender 1 is 1, -1, 1, -1, 1, -1, 1, and 1. The 8-bit CDMA code for sender 2 is 1, 1, 1, -1, 1, 1, -1, and -1, as shown in the figure below. Sender 1 has two data bits to send: a 1 followed by a -1; sender 2 also has two data bits to send: a -1 followed by a 1. Compute the sequence of mini-slot bits sent into the channel by sender 1 and by sender 2. Also compute the combined bit values on the channel. The figure below shows the first two mini-slot bits sent by each sender, and the first two mini-slot combined bits values in the channel. You should compute the values for the remaining 14 mini-slots, that is, for the gray-shaded regions in the figure to the right.

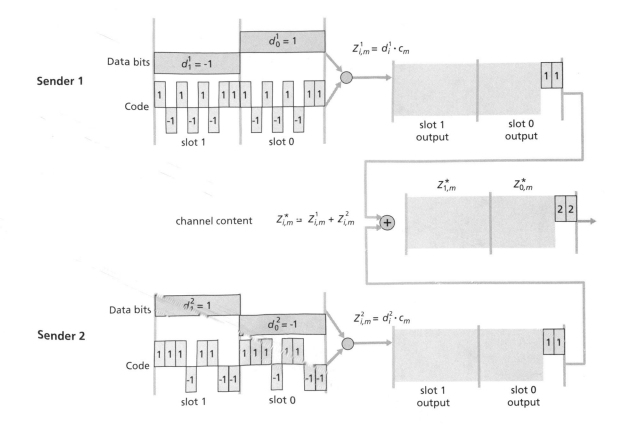

3.   **A multi-receiver CDMA example.** This problem builds on the answer to the previous problem; you'll need to use the answer to the previous problem to do this problem. Assume now that there are two receivers. Receiver 1 wants to obtain the two data bits sent from sender 1 and knows sender 1's CDMA code; similarly, receiver 2 wants to receive the two data bits sent from sender 2 and knows sender 2's CDMA code. Both receivers receive the 16 mini-slotted bits in the combined channel, that is, the sum of the mini-slotted bits sent by sender 1 and sender 2. These 16 bits are shown in the three leftmost grey-shaded boxes in the figure below (all three boxes contain this same 16-bit sequence). Perform the CDMA decoding operation for each receiver, that is, calculate the values of d_i^1 and d_i^2 shown in the figure below. This will show you that a receiver can indeed calculate the original bits sent by the sender in which it is interested.

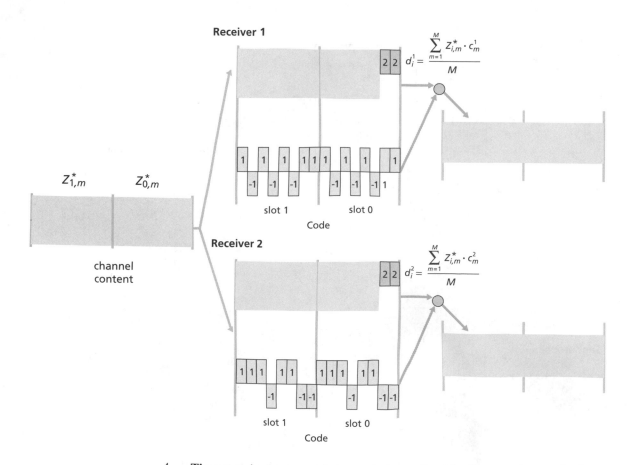

4.   **Time-varying access point associations.** Consider the scenario described on page 516 of the textbook, in which you enter a Wi-Fi jungle in a café with your laptop, a blueberry muffin, and many Wi-Fi networks with which your laptop's wireless interface can associate. Suppose that your laptop associates with the access point with the strongest signal. Suppose also that the signal strengths of the access points vary over time, so your association will also change over time. We are interested in the effects of a changing link-level association, and the consequent change of IP address when an association changes.

   a.   Suppose that initially your access point association changes relatively slowly over time, and that you are browsing the web using HTTP 1.0, and only occasionally downloading Web pages. Is the changing link-layer association and change of IP address likely to be a problem for you?

   b.   Now suppose that you want to perform a file transfer over TCP that is so large that it is likely that your laptop's link-level association will change during the file transfer. Is the changing link-layer association and consequent change of IP address likely to be an issue for you?

5. **802.11 networks using different channels.** Let us return to Review Question 1. We learned on page 516 of the textbook that an 802.11 network can choose to operate using any of the 11 different available channels (frequency bands). Consider again the figure shown in Review Question 1. Can you assign channels to nodes such that the wireless network achieves the same throughput as in the wired case? (Note: you may assume that each node has two interfaces, with each interface having a different channel).

6. **802.11 ACK timeout values.** Certain 802.11 implementations use a fixed ACK timeout value, with a default value that is set for indoor (for example, less than 100 meters) communication. The timeout value determines the amount of time that the 802.11 sender will wait for an ACK frame after sending a DATA frame. If the ACK does not arrive within this amount of time, the DATA frame is assumed to be lost, and the DATA frame will be retransmitted. Suppose we want to use 802.11 with an outdoor, long-distance directional antenna that can transmit over a distance of say, 5 miles. What do you think will happen if the ACK timeout value remains set for the 100 m indoor case?

7. **RTS/CTS.** Consider the scenario shown below, in which node D sends an RTS to node C at t_0. Node C responds to the RTS with a CTS (which is heard by nodes B and C) in accordance with 802.11 protocol, and node D begins the transmission of its message at t_2. In the meantime, node A sends an RTS message to B at time t_1.

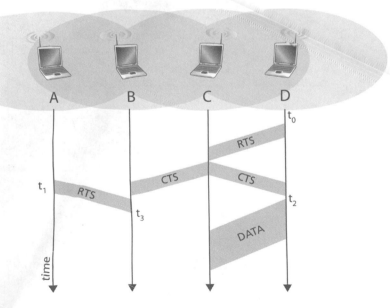

a. If node A were to begin transmitting to node B at some point after t_3, would A's transmission be successfully received at B?

b. If node A were to begin transmitting to node B at some point after t_3, would A's transmission interfere with the ongoing transmission from D-to-C?

c. At t_3, can B respond to A's RTS message with a CTS message? Why or why not?

8. **DIFS and SIFS timing in 802.11.** The SIFS is the amount of time that a node waits between receiving a DATA frame and sending an ACK. The DIFS is the amount of time that a node waits (sensing the medium) before sending a new DATA frame. Why do you think that the designers of 802.11 made the SIFS shorter than the DIFS?

9. **Mobile IP: indirection and encapsulation.** Consider the scenario below in which a mobile node whose permanent address in its home network is 128.119.40.186, is visiting a foreign network and has received a care-of-address of 79.129.13.2. A correspondent with address 102.67.7.8 sends a UDP segment to the mobile host using Mobile IP. Consider the IP datagrams A, B, and C. What are the source and destination IP addresses of these datagrams? Also, describe the contents of the payload (data) part of these IP datagrams.

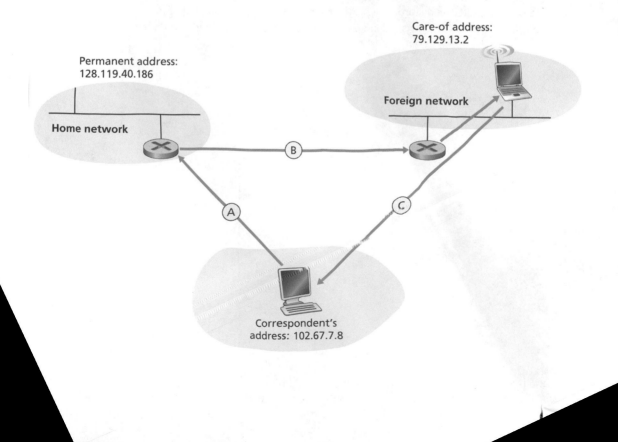

10. **Packet loss during handoff.** Consider the mobile IP scenario in Review Question 9. The round trip time (RTT) between the correspondent and the home network is 1000 ms; the RTT between the home network and the foreign network is 120 ms. There is also a second foreign network (not shown in the figure above) that has an RTT from the home network of 160 ms. You may assume that all delays are fixed, and that the one-way delays between two points is equal to one-half the RTT. The correspondent is sending datagrams to the mobile hosts at a rate of one packet every 100 ms, periodically, and has been sending such datagrams for a long time (that is, long before t = 0). Suppose that the home network receives datagrams from the correspondent at t = 0, 100, 200, 300, and so on. At t = 100, the mobile node leaves the first foreign network and 500 msec later joins the second foreign network.

   a. Suppose that the mobile node leaves the first foreign network without signaling this to the foreign agent, and then joins the second foreign network at which time the mobile IP registration process begins between the foreign agent in the new network and the home agent. Are any of the datagrams being relayed by the home agent to the mobile node lost during the mobile node's transition between foreign networks? Explain.

   b. Suppose now that the RTT delay between the home network and each of the foreign networks is doubled. How many datagram will be lost?

   c. Suppose that the RTTs between the home and foreign networks are the same as in the initial problem statement. Now suppose that the delay between the correspondent and the home network is doubled. How many datagrams will be lost?

   d. Now suppose that when the mobile node leaves the initial foreign network at t = 100, it informs the foreign agent in this original foreign network. This foreign agent then informs the home agent that the mobile node is leaving the foreign network and that it (the home agent) should buffer any packets it receives from the correspondent until a registration is received from a new foreign agent, at which point the buffered packets can be sent to the mobile host in the new foreign network. In this scenario, (i) how many packets are lost, assuming that once a packet is sent, it can not be retransmitted, and (ii) how many packets are buffered at the home agent?

Answers to Review Questions

1. a. Note that A must send to B, B must send to C, and C must send to D. Also note that C's transmissions to D are heard by B, and thus B cannot receive from A (nor can B send to C) while C is transmitting to D, since A's and C's message would interfere at B. Similarly, neither A nor C can transmit when B is transmitting. Thus, only one node can ever be transmitting during a time slot. Since each message must be transmitted over three hops (A-B, B-C, and C-D), the maximum rate at which messages can be transmitted from A to D is one message every three time slots, or 0.3333 messages/slot.

    b. Message transmissions can now be pipelined, while A is sending to B, B can be sending to C, and C can be sending to D. The maximum rate is thus one message/slot (three times the throughput of the wireless scenario!).

    c. Consider the following sequence of transmissions, in which data message flow from left to right, and ACK messages flow from right to left. Each line below shows the transmission activity during a time slot.

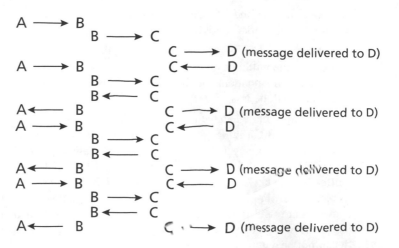

    Note that here we are able to take advantage of spatial reuse of the wireless channel: A can send a data message to B at the same time that an ACK is being sent to from D to C. Similarly, C can send a data message to D at the same time that B is sending an ACK message to A. The throughput is thus one message every four slots, or 0.25 messages/slot.

2.

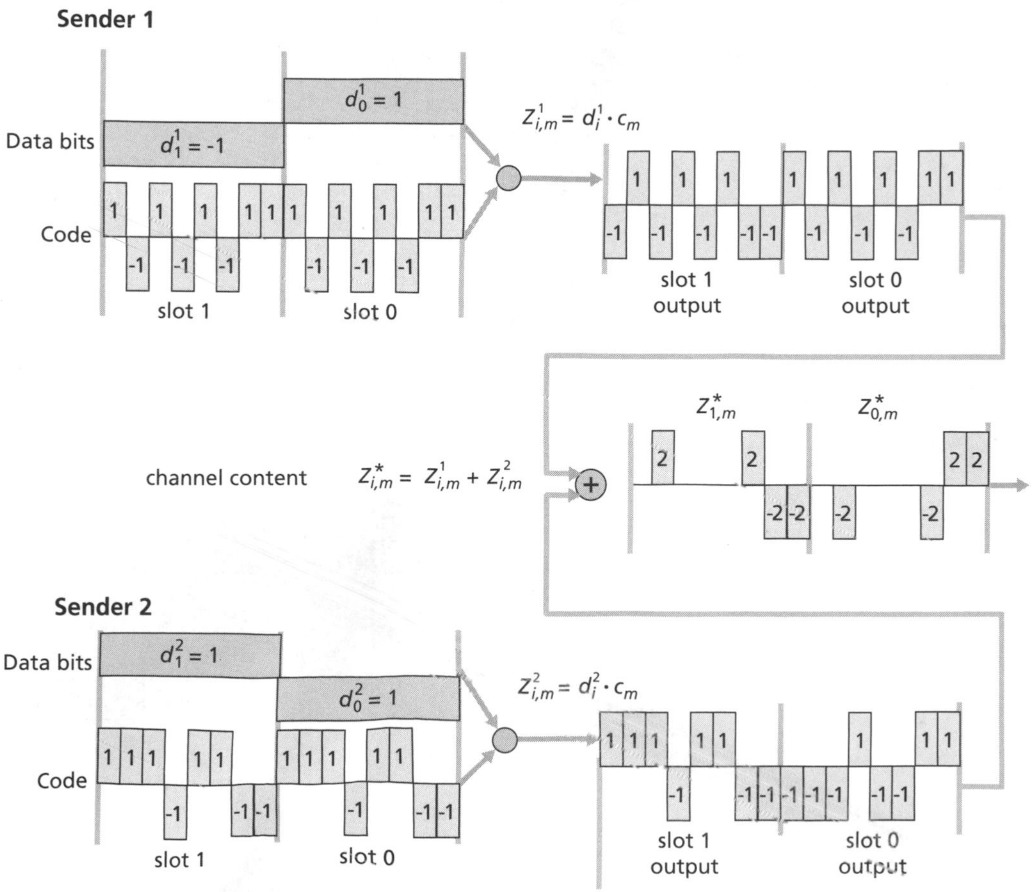

Sender 1

Data bits

$d_0^1 = 1$

$d_1^1 = -1$

$Z_{i,m}^1 = d_i^1 \cdot c_m$

Code

slot 1   slot 0

slot 1 output   slot 0 output

channel content $Z_{i,m}^* = Z_{i,m}^1 + Z_{i,m}^2$

$Z_{1,m}^*$ $Z_{0,m}^*$

Sender 2

Data bits $d_1^2 = 1$

$d_0^2 = 1$

$Z_{i,m}^2 = d_i^2 \cdot c_m$

Code

slot 1   slot 0

slot 1 output   slot 0 output

3.

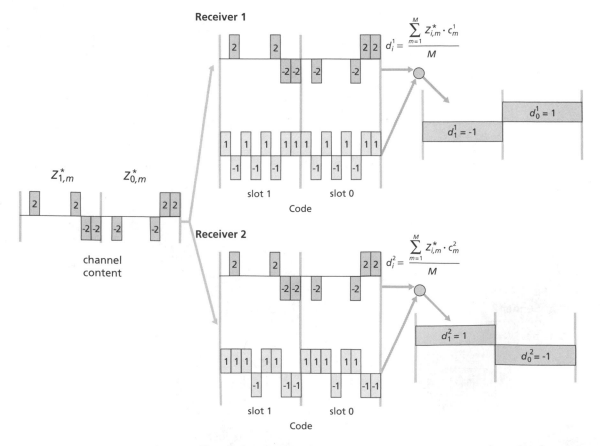

4. a. Recall that HTTP 1.0 Web transfers are transaction-oriented and non-persistent. Thus, as long as your link layer association does not change while you are downloading a page, the changing link-layer association will not be visible to your web browser application.

   b. If your laptop's link-layer association changes, your laptop will need an IP address in the network associated with the new access point. This network is likely to be different from the network associated with the old access point. Thus, your IP address is likely to change, and you will no longer be receiving datagrams sent to your old IP address. If a file transfer is in progress when your link-layer association changes, the file transfer will eventually abort because the underlying TCP sender will no longer receive ACKs from your laptop, once your laptop joins the new network and discards its old IP address.

5. Let us assign 802.11 channel 1 to node A, channel 6 to node B, and channel 11 to node C. Node A will send on channel 1; node B will receive on channel 1 and send on channel 6; node C will listen on channel 6, and send on channel 11; and node D will listen on channel 11. In this case, the channels do not interfere with each other, and messages can be transmitted simultaneously on any of the channels. In this case, the 802.11 network achieves the same throughput as in the wired case.

6. If the ACK timeout value is set too short, the sender will timeout prematurely, before an ACK has a chance to propagate back to the sender. In this case, the sender may retry its transmission (thereby interfering with the returning ACK), or simply ignore the late-arriving ACK. One of the authors actually learned this lesson the hard way, when working with a class of undergraduates on outdoor 802.11 networks. See http://madwifi.org/wiki/UserDocs/LongDistance for an interesting discussion of 802.11 issues over long distance links.

7. *a.* Yes. A's message would be received successfully at B since D's transmission does not reach B.

   b. No. A's transmission would not interfere with D's transmission at C, since A's transmission does not reach C.

   c. No. B cannot respond to A's RTS. When B receives the CTS from C, it (B) must defer its transmission until after the DATA frame sent by D and the ACK message (not shown) sent by C have been sent. Thus, B cannot respond to A's RTS and thus, A cannot send, even though its message transmission would be correctly received at B and would not interfere with the transmission from D to C.

8. Suppose at any given time, a node has a new DATA frame to send and begins waiting for DIFS time units. At the same time, a nearby node has just successfully received a DATA frame. In this case, the latter node will transmit its ACK after waiting only SIFS time units, that is, before the node with the new DATA frame begins its transmission of its DATA frame. Thus, the smaller value of SIFS gives priority to nodes wanting to send an ACK over nodes wanting to send a new DATA frame.

9. • Datagram A has source address of 102.67.7.8 and a destination address of 128.119.40.186. The payload of datagram A is the UDP segment being sent from the correspondent to the mobile host.

   • Datagram B has a source address of the IP address of the home agent, and a destination address of 79.129.13.2 The payload of datagram B is datagram A.

   • Datagram C has a source address of 79.129.13.2, and a destination address of 102.67.7.8. The payload of datagram C is whatever reply the mobile host sends to the correspondent.

10. a. The mobile arrives at the foreign network at t = 600 msec and immediately registers with the foreign agent who then immediately sends a new registration to the home agent. This registration arrives at the home agent at t = 680 msec. When the next datagram arrives from the correspondent at t = 700, the home agent will then relay this to the mobile in the new foreign network. The datagrams sent at t = 100, 200, 300, 400, 500, and 600 will have been sent to the original foreign network. The mobile node will have already left the foreign network when these datagrams arrive, and so these six datagrams will be lost.

b. In this case, the registration message from the new foreign network arrives at the home agent at t = 760, and so seven messages will have been sent to the old foreign network, and hence, lost.

c. Trick question! The answer is six, following exactly the same reasoning as in 10(a). Note that even with an increase in delay between the correspondent and the home network, datagrams will still be arriving at t = 100, 200, 300, 400, 500, 600, and so on.

d. The de-registration message arrives at the home network at t = 180 msec, and so the datagram sent at t = 100 will be lost. The home agent will buffer the packets arriving from the correspondent at t = 200, 300, 400, 500, and 600 and forward these to the mobile host when it (the home agent) receives the new registration at t = 680 msec. Thus, one datagram is lost, and five are buffered and eventually sent.

Multimedia Networking

Most Important Ideas and Concepts from Chapter 7

♦ **Differences (and similarities) among the requirements of streaming stored multimedia, streaming live multimedia, and real-time interactive multimedia.** In Section 7.1, we identified three classes of multimedia applications: *streaming stored multimedia, streaming live multimedia,* and *real-time interactive multimedia.* (We also identified but ignored, a fourth case in which a stored multimedia file is downloaded in its entirety and then played out, as this case is simply a file transfer application.) In all three cases, multimedia data has both content (for example, the bytes that make up an audio sample or a video frame) and timing attributes. The timing attribute of a video frame might be its temporal location during a particular 1/30 of a second interval of time in the video. Similarly, a packet audio stream might consist of chunks of audio data gathered every 20 msec; the timing attribute of an audio chunk might then be its temporal location within a sequential stream of audio chunks.

Stored applications have the flexibility to transmit data as fast as the network path will allow, since all of the multimedia is stored and always available for transmission. Live applications do not have this flexibility. Interactive human-to-human communication (for example, a teleconference or an audio call) requires low end-end latencies, typically less than 400 msec in order for such interaction communication to feel "natural" for the participants.

♦ **Playout delay for jitter removal.** When multimedia data is transferred over a network to a receiver for playout, the receiver must playout the data according to the data's original timing attributes (see "Differences (and similarities) among the requirements of streaming stored multimedia, streaming live multimedia, and real-time interactive multimedia" above). For example, audio and video data might need to be played out periodically at the receiver, for example, at a rate of one video frame every 1/30 sec, or one audio sample every 20 msec. Once playout begins, the remaining pieces of data each have a playout time that depends on its timing attribute. Data not received before their playout time are considered lost. Another challenge in networked multimedia is that network transmission results in variable delays—jitter—in the received data. For example, data transmitted periodically typically will not arrive periodically. This network-induced jitter must not be apparent in the multimedia playout at the receiver.

One technique to decrease the amount of late-arriving data *and to accommodate* jitter is to delay the beginning of playout, essentially pushing the playout deadlines further into the future. In this case, pieces of arriving data are placed in a playout buffer. After some initial playout delay, the playout process begins and pieces of data are removed from the buffer as dictated by their original timing attributes. The playout buffer not only decreases late-arrival loss, but also masks the jitter. For example, if there are ten packets of data in the playout buffer, it is irrelevant whether those ten packets arrived smoothly over time (with no jitter) or arrived with wildly different delays (high jitter).

♦ **Forward error correction (FEC).** In Chapter 3, we studied a number of reliable data transfer protocols that retransmitted lost or damaged packets. An alternative approach toward achieving reliability is to use *forward error correction* techniques. With FEC, enough redundant information is added to the original data so that even if some of the transmitted data (original data plus redundant data) is lost, the receiver can still recover the original data. The simple two-dimensional parity technique that we studied in Chapter 5 for detection and correction of single bit errors is a simple example of FEC. FEC techniques can be particularly valuable when an application cannot wait for a round-trip time to recover lost data via a timeout-and-transmit mechanism.

♦ **The Real-Time Transport Protocol (RTP).** RTP is an Internet-standard protocol for the transport of real-time data such as multimedia. It can be used for streaming stored multimedia, streaming live multimedia, and real-time interactive multimedia. RTP does not itself provide for resource reservation, call admission, or quality of service control; these tasks are left to RSVP and other protocols (see "Intserv, Diffserv, and RSVP" below). Instead, RTP provides information (carried both in RTP packet headers, as well as via a separate control protocol known as RTCP) to help the senders and receivers of RTP data perform tasks such as timing reconstruction (see "Playout delay for jitter removal" above), loss detection, content identification, and synchronization among multiple multimedia streams.

♦ **The Session Initiation Protocol (SIP).** In telephone networks, so-called signaling protocols have been used for decades to control the manner in which telephone calls are initiated, end-points (for example, the phone associated with an individual subscriber number or the service point for an 800 call) are located, endpoints are contacted, and the circuit through the network connecting the endpoint is set up. SIP is an Internet-standards-track signaling protocol for Internet telephony, teleconferencing, instant messaging, and more. Key elements of the SIP architecture include SIP proxies (which help locate remote endpoints and direct calls to these endpoints), and SIP registrars (which keep track of the locations of registered users). As a more recently-developed protocol, SIP's design reflects many of the best aspects of earlier protocols, such as HTTP, DNS, and Mobile IP.

♦ **High-quality multimedia applications *are* possible over today's best-effort network.** During the 1990s, a considerable amount of networking research was devoted toward developing a new network architecture (see "Beyond best effort: packet classification, isolation among traffic flows, and resource reservation" below) that would provide quality of service (QoS) guarantees to multimedia applications. However, the astounding success of multimedia applications such as Skype demonstrates that it *is* possible to run multimedia applications over today's best-effort public Internet, a network architecture that provides no explicit QoS support. Certainly, as long as resources (for example, bandwidth) are plentiful, multimedia applications can indeed operate effectively over today's Internet. Application-layer techniques such as adaptive playout buffering, FEC, loss masking, and adaptive coding rates that match the coding rate to the available bandwidth can improve application-layer performance when the network becomes congested. However, these techniques can compensate for scarce bandwidth only up to a certain point; beyond that, the quality of the multimedia applications will inevitably degrade as the network becomes more congested. So, the question remains—are new network mechanisms and new network architectures required to support multimedia applications? In the end, the answer to this question is likely to be determined more by economics than by technology. If bandwidth remains relatively plentiful and multimedia users are willing to put up with the (hopefully occasional) poor performance when the network is congested, then multimedia over a best-effort Internet may well be the direction in which future networked multimedia activity grows.

♦ **Beyond best effort: packet classification, isolation among traffic flows, and resource reservation.** An alternative to continuing to run multimedia applications over today's best-effort Internet (see "High quality multimedia applications are possible over today's best-effort network" above) is to develop a new network architecture that provides explicit QoS support for multimedia applications. In such a network, once a multimedia call is admitted to the network, it receives a guarantee that it will receive a given quality of service (for example, a bounded end-end delay and packet loss rate) throughout the duration of the call. This service model is similar to that of the telephone network—either a call is admitted to the network with a guaranteed QoS or the call is rejected (that is, the user receives a "busy signal" from the network) and the user must try the call again, when the network is hopefully less congested. In Section 7.6, we identified several key architectural components of a future QoS-enabled network, including packet classification, isolation among traffic flows, and resource reservation. Indeed, these concepts are already embodied in a number of Internet RFCs and protocols, including Intserv, Diffserv, and RSVP, as discussed in Sections 7.8 and 7.9, and "Intserv, Diffserv, and RSVP" below.

♦ **Scheduling disciplines: FIFO, Round Robin, Priority, and WFQ.** Buried deep within every Internet router and host, in the guts of the link layer, is a very important construct—the queue (buffer) of frames waiting to be forwarded across the link to the device at the other end of the link. The manner in which queued packets are selected for transmission across this link—the link scheduling discipline—has a tremendous impact on application performance. We studied four packet scheduling disciplines in this chapter: FIFO (in which packets are transmitted in their order of arrival), priority service (in which packets are divided into classes, with packets from a higher priority class being transmitted before queued packets from a lower priority class), Round Robin (where packets are again divided into classes, with each class receiving a turn to transmit a packet from that class), and Weighted Fair Queuing (a generalization of Round Robin, with different classes of traffic being given a different number of turns to transmit a packet).

♦ **Policing: the leaky bucket mechanism.** In today's best-effort Internet, there are no constraints (other than the physical link speed) on how fast a user (say using the UDP transport protocol) can send packets into the network. For example, if N-1 users are each sending packets to their first hop router at rate R, an Nth user is free to send packets at rate 5R, or indeed any rate. A leaky bucket mechanism limits both the long term rate at which packets can be sent into the network (given by the leaky bucket's token rate, r, shown in Figure 7.29 on page 626 of the textbook) and the so-called burstiness of packet transmission (given by the size of the token bucket, b, in Figure 7.29, which limits the maximum number of packets that can be sent into the network in a short period of time to a maximum of b packets). A policing mechanism such as the leaky bucket is important for providing QoS guarantees because it limits the amount of traffic that an individual user can send into the network, thereby providing a degree of isolation among users.

♦ **Intserv, Diffserv, and RSVP.** The integrated service (Intserv) and differentiated services (Diffserv) architectures are the two network architectures developed within the Internet community to provide QoS guarantees to network applications. Intserv provides the framework for providing hard guarantees (for example, a maximum guaranteed end-end delay) to a session via resource reservation and call admission/blocking. The call admission decision is based on the network's ability to meet the session's requested QoS without violating QoS guarantees made to existing sessions that have already been admitted to the network. Diffserv provides performance guarantees among classes of traffic, rather than to individual sessions. Both Intserv and Diffserv need a signaling protocol to convey information about the traffic demands and performance requirements of individual sessions (in the case of Intserv) or classes of traffic (in the case of Diffserv). This is one of the roles of the Resource Reservation Protocol (RSVP). We would be remiss if we did not mention that Asynchronous Transfer Mode (ATM) networks were also designed to provide QoS guarantees. For example, we saw in Table 4.1 on page 306 of the textbook, that ATM provides a class of service with even stronger guarantees than the Internet Intserv model—ATM's constant bit rate (CBR) service class not only provides a bandwidth guarantee, but also promises to maintain the inter-packet timing of packets flowing through a CBR connection!

Review Questions

This section provides additional study questions. Answers to each question are provided in the next section.

1. **End-end delay versus delay jitter.** What is the difference between end-end delay and delay jitter? Which of these (delay or delay jitter) is ameliorated with the use of a playout buffer? Suppose that packet audio is transmitted periodically. If the end-end delay is very large, but the jitter is zero, would a large or small playout buffer be needed?

2. **Packet audio playout.** Consider the figure below (which is similar to Figure 7.6 on page 588 of the textbook). A sender begins sending packetized audio periodically at t = 1. The first packet arrives at the receiver at t = 8.

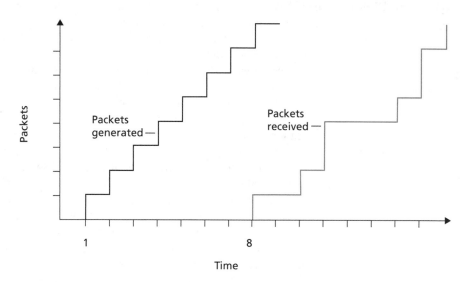

a. What are the delays (from sender to receiver, ignoring any playout delays) of the second, third, fourth, and fifth packets sent? Note that each vertical and horizontal line segment in the figure has a length of 1, 2, or 3 time units.

b. If audio playout begins as soon as the first packet arrives at the receiver at t = 8, which of the first 8 packets sent will *not* arrive in time for playout?

c. If audio playout begins at t = 9, which of the first 8 packets sent will *not* arrive in time for playout?

d. What is the minimum playout delay at the receiver that results in all of the first 8 packets arriving in time for playout?

3. **Estimating delay and delay deviation.** Consider the figure from Review Question 2 showing packet audio transmission and reception times.

   a. Compute the estimated delay for packets 2 through 8, using the formula for d_i on page 589 of the textbook. Use a value of $u = 0.1$.

   b. Compute the estimated deviation of the delay from the estimated average for packets 2 through 8, using the formula for v_i on page 589 of the textbook. Use a value of $u = 0.1$.

4. **ACKs versus FEC.** Consider a sender and receiver that are separated by a long-distance, high-bandwidth link that can occasionally lose or damage packets. The link is running at low utilization, and it is important to keep the application-to-application delivery delay as small as possible. Would you recommend using an acknowledgement-based mechanism or an FEC-based mechanism for reliable data transfer? Why?

5. **RTP.** Why do you think RTP has both a timestamp field and a sequence number field? For example, in order to recover from loss, if the receiver knows that the packetization interval is 20 msec, and receives packets with timestamps of 0, 20, 40, 60, and 100 msec, isn't that sufficient to know that the sample taken at 80 msec has been lost?

6. **Similarities and differences between SIP and Mobile IP.** Comment on the similarities and differences between how SIP and Mobile IP support communication between two (potentially mobile) devices.

7. **Packet scheduling.** Consider the following figure, which is similar to Figures 7.24–7.27 on pages 622–624 of the textbook.

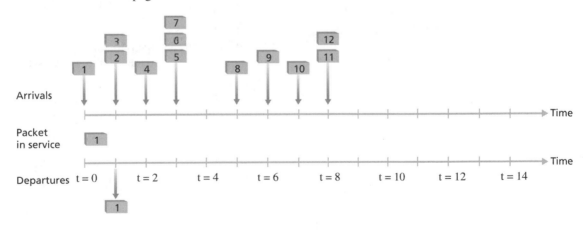

   a. Assuming FIFO service, indicate the time at which packets 2 through 12 each leave the queue. For each packet, what is the delay between its arrival and the beginning of the slot in which it is transmitted? What is the average of this delay over all 12 packets?

b. Now assume a Priority Service, and assume that odd-numbered packets are high priority, and even-numbered packets are low priority. Indicate the time at which packets 2 through 12 each leave the queue. For each packet, what is the delay between its arrival and the beginning of the slot in which it is transmitted? What is the average of this delay over all 12 packets?

c. Now assume Round Robin service. Assume that packets 1, 2, 3, 6, 11, and 12 are from class 1, and packets 4, 5, 7, 8, 9, and 10 are from class 2. Indicate the time at which packets 2 through 12 each leave the queue. For each packet, what is the delay between its arrival and the beginning of the time slot in which it is transmitted? What is the average delay over all 12 packets?

d. Now assume Weighted Fair Queuing (WFQ) service. Assume that odd-numbered packets are from class 1, and even-numbered packets are from class 2. Class 1 has a WFQ weight of 2, while class 2 has a WFQ weight of 1. Note that it may not be possible to achieve an idealized WFQ schedule as described in the textbook, so indicate why you have chosen the particular packet to go into service at each time slot. For each packet, what is the delay between its arrival and the beginning of the time slot in which it is transmitted? What is the average delay over all 12 packets?

e. What do you notice about the average delay in all four cases (FCFS, RR, Priority, and WFQ)?

8. **Packet scheduling (more).** Consider again the figure from Review Question 7.

a. Assume a priority service, with packets 1, 4, 5, 6, and 11 being high priority packets. The remaining packets are low priority. Indicate the slots in which packets 2 through 12 each leave the queue.

b. Now suppose that round robin-service is used, with packets 1, 4, 5, 6, and 11 belonging to one class of traffic, and the remaining packets belonging to the second class of traffic. Indicate the slots in which packets 2 through 12 each leave the queue.

c. Now suppose that WFQ service is used, with packets 1, 4, 5, 6, and 11 belonging to one class of traffic, and the remaining packets belonging to the second class of traffic. Class 1 has a WFQ weight of 1, while class 2 has a WFQ weight of 2 (note that these weights are different from those in Review Question 7). Indicate the slots in which packets 2 through 12 each leave the queue. See also the caveat in the question 7d above regarding WFQ service.

9. **Leaky bucket.** Consider the following figure, which shows a leaky bucket policer being fed by a stream of packets. The token buffer can hold at most two tokens, and is initially full at t = 0. New tokens arrive at a rate of 1 token per slot. The output link speed is such that if two packets obtain tokens at the beginning of a time slot, they can both pass to the output link in the same slot. The timing details of the system are as follows:

1. Packets (if any) arrive at the beginning of the slot. Thus, in the example below, packets 1 and 2 arrive in slot 0. If there are already packets in the queue, then the arriving packets join the end of the queue. Packets proceed toward the front of the queue in a FIFO manner.

2. If, after the arrivals (if any) have been added to the queue, there are any queued packets, one or two of those packets (depending on the number of available tokens) will each remove a token from the token buffer and pass to the output link during that slot. Thus, as shown in the example below, packets 0 and 1 each remove a token from the buffer (since there are initially two tokens) and pass to the output link during slot 0.

3. A new token is added to the token buffer if it is not full, since the token generation rate is r = 1 token/slot.

4. Time then advances to the next time slot, and these steps repeat.

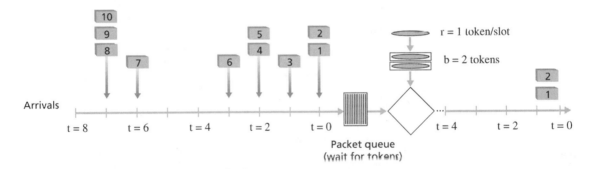

a. For each time slot, identify the packets that are in the queue and the number of tokens in the bucket, immediately after the arrivals have been processed (see step 1 above) but before any of the packets have passed through the queue and removed a token. Thus, for the t = 0 time slot in the example above, packets 1 and 2 are in the queue, and there are two tokens in the buffer.

b. For each time slot, indicate which packets appear on the output after the token(s) have been removed from the queue. Thus, for the t = 0 time slot in the example above, packets 1 and 2 appear on the output link from the leaky buffer during slot 0.

10. **Leaky bucket (more).** Repeat Review Question 9, but assume that r = 2. Assume again that the bucket is initially full.

11. **Leaky bucket (even more).** Consider Review Question 10 and suppose that r = 3, and that b = 2 as before. Will your answer to the question above change?

Answers to Review Questions

1. The end-end delay of a packet is the total accumulated delay from when the packet is sent by the sender to when it is received at the final destination, including propagation, queuing, and forwarding delays at the intervening routers on the end-end path. Delay jitter refers to the difference in end-end delay between two adjacent packets. The playout buffer is used to remove the jitter from the received audio packets, so that packets can be played out according to their original timing attributes. If there was no delay jitter, periodically-transmitted packets would arrive periodically with their inter-packet timing preserved, and hence there would be no need for a playout buffer (regardless of the end-end delay).

2. a. The delay of packet 2 is 8 slots. The delay of packet 3 is 8 slots. The delay of packet 4 is 7 slots. The delay of packet 5 is 9 slots.

   b. Packets 2, 3, 5, 6, 7, and 8 will not be received in time for their playout if playout begins at $t = 8$.

   c. Packets 5 and 6 will not be received in time for their playout if playout begins at $t = 9$.

   d. No packets will arrive after their playout time if playout begins at $t = 10$.

3. The answers to parts a and b are in the table below.

Packet Number	$r_i - t_i$	d_i	v_i
1	7	7	0
2	8	7.10	0.09
3	8	7.19	0.162
4	7	7.17	0.163
5	9	7.35	0.311
6	9	7.52	0.428
7	8	7.57	0.429
8	8	7.61	0.425

4. An FEC-based mechanism would be a good idea here, since the utilization is low, FEC bits can be used to correct an error (and even a lost packet) at the receiver without having to wait a round-trip time to timeout and re-transmit the data in error.

5. If there is no multimedia data generated during the interval beginning at 80 msec (for example, the audio source is in a silent period), then (depending on the audio application) it is possible that no packet would be sent. With sequence

numbers, the fact that there was no audio sample at 80 msec would be clear, since the audio sample at 100 msec would have a sequence number that is only one larger than the sample taken at 60 msec (indicating that there was no sample at 80 msec). Without the sequence number, the receiver would not know whether there was simply no data generated during the 80 msec interval (for example, silence) or whether data was generated but the packet containing the data was lost.

6. Similarities:

- The idea of a registrar—a place that one can go to get information about the location of a user—is similar to the home agent in Mobile IP. However, a user may be registered with multiple SIP registrars (as shown in Figure 7.14 on page 608 of the textbook), and so a SIP proxy may need to contact several registrars before locating a user. In this respect, SIP location resolution is somewhat closer to DNS name resolution than Mobile IP user location. In mobile IP there is only a single home agent.
- In both Mobile IP and in SIP, a mobile user will register with its home agent or SP registrar so that the agent/registrar knows its location.

Differences:

- In Mobile IP, all communication to the mobile host goes through the home agent. In SIP, once the SIP clients have each other's address, communication in both directions is directly between the clients, without additionally involving the SIP proxy or registrar.

7. a.

FCFS Service			
Packet	Arrival slot	Transmission slot	Delay
1	0	0	0
2	1	1	0
3	1	2	1
4	2	3	1
5	3	4	1
6	3	5	2
7	3	6	3
8	5	7	2
9	6	8	2
10	7	9	2
11	8	10	2
12	8	11	3
		Average delay:	1.583

b.

		Priority Service		
Packet	Class	Arrival slot	Transmission slot	Delay
1	H	0	0	0
2	L	1	2	1
3	H	1	1	0
4	L	2	5	3
5	H	3	3	0
6	L	3	7	4
7	H	3	4	1
8	L	5	9	4
9	H	6	6	0
10	L	7	10	3
11	H	8	8	0
12	L	8	11	3
			Average delay:	1.583

c.

		Round Robin Service		
Packet	Class	Arrival slot	Transmission slot	Delay
1	C1	0	0	0
2	C1	1	1	0
3	C1	1	3	2
4	C2	2	2	0
5	C2	3	4	1
6	C1	3	5	2
7	C2	3	6	3
8	C2	5	7	2
9	C2	6	9	3
10	C2	7	11	4
11	C1	8	8	0
12	C1	8	10	2
			Average delay:	1.583

d. In this solution, we implement WFQ by dividing time into sets of three arrivals slots (0–2, 3–5, 6–8, 9–11). For each set of arrival slots, we consider the packets that are available for transmission during those three slots. We try to transmit two packets from class 1 and one packet from class 2 during these three slots. By convention, class 1 packets go before class 2 packets within this group of three, when possible.

In slots 0–2, it is possible to transmit two class 1 packets (packets 1, 3) and one class 2 packet (packet 2). During slots 3–5, it is possible to send two class 1 packets (packets 5, 7) and one class 2 packet (packet 4). During slots 6–8, it is possible to send only one class 1 packet (9), so we send two class 2 packets (6, 8) after sending packet 9 (assuming that once we begin sending class 2 packets during a set of three slots, we only send class 2 packets from then on). In slots 9–11, there is only one more class 1 packet to send (11), so we send it, followed by the last two class 2 packets (10, 12).

WFQ Service				
Packet	Class	Arrival slot	Transmission slot	Delay
1	C1	0	0	0
2	C2	1	2	1
3	C1	1	1	0
4	C2	2	5	3
5	C1	3	3	0
6	C2	3	7	4
7	C1	3	4	1
8	C2	5	8	3
9	C1	6	6	0
10	C2	7	10	3
11	C1	8	9	1
12	C2	8	11	3
			Average delay:	1.583

e. The average delay of a packet is the same in all cases! This illustrates an important conservation law of queuing systems: as long as the queue is kept busy whenever there is a packet queued, the average packet delay will be the same, regardless of the scheduling discipline! Of course, specific packets will suffer higher or lower delays under different scheduling disciplines, but the average will always be the same.

8. The answers to parts a–c are in the table below.

Packet	Class	Arrival slot	Transmission slot under Priority	Transmission slot under RR	Transmission slot under WFQ
1	C1	0	0	0	0
2	C2	1	1	1	1
3	C2	1	5	3	2
4	C1	2	2	2	3
5	C1	3	3	4	6
6	C1	3	4	6	9
7	C2	3	6	5	4
8	C2	5	7	7	5
9	C2	6	9	9	7
10	C2	7	10	10	8
11	C1	8	8	8	10
12	C2	8	11	11	11

9. The answers to parts a and b can be found in the table below.

Slot	Packets in queue	Number of tokens before output	Packets on oputput
0	1, 2	2	1, 2
1	3	1	3
2	4, 5	1	4
3	5, 6	1	5
4	6	1	6
5	empty	1	
6	7	2	7
7	8, 9, 10	2	8, 9
8	10	1	10

10.

Slot	Packets in queue	Number of tokens before output	Packets on output
0	1, 2	2	1, 2
1	3	2	3
2	4, 5	2	4, 5
3	6	2	6
4	empty	2	
5	empty	2	
6	7	2	7
7	8, 9, 10	2	8, 9
8	10	3	10

11.   No. Since the bucket can only hold two tokens, one of the arriving three to-kens will overflow and be lost. Thus, at most, two tokens can actually enter the bucket per slot, which is the same condition as in Review Question 10.

Security

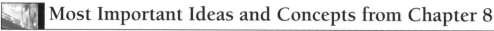 Most Important Ideas and Concepts from Chapter 8

♦ **Networks are vulnerable to attacks.** Computer networks, and in particular the Internet, are vulnerable to a wide array of attacks. These attacks include the following:

- **Sniffing:** Also known as eavesdropping and wire tapping, the act of sniffing is to make copies of packets as they travel across a link. The packets can then be examined for sensitive information. It is trivial to sniff packets sent over a wireless LAN; sniffing packets sent between Alice and Bob over a wired link can be more challenging. If the nodes in an Ethernet LAN are interconnected with a hub, then sniffing is straightforward; however, if they are interconnected with a switch, then sniffing is difficult (but not impossible). The primary defense against sniffing is encryption.

- **Modification, insertion, and deletion of message content:** Even more insidious than sniffing, here the attacker modifies the transmitted data without either of the communicating entities being aware of it. This can be done by flipping bits, inserting bits or packets, or deleting bits or packets. As described in the chapter, the primary defenses against data modification are message digests, sequence numbers, and encryption.

- **Masquerading:** The attacker pretends to be something that it is not (a person, a router interface, and so on). For example, Trudy may pretend to be Alice, who normally is trusted by Bob. Trudy can then send commands to Bob—who thinking that the commands come from trustworthy Alice—executes the commands. Or Trudy, masquerading as Alice, may be able to extract sensitive information from Bob. As described in the chapter, defenses for masquerading include handshaking, certificates, nonces, and message digests.

- **Network mapping:** Before attacking a particular network, such as a corporate network, often attackers would like to know the IP addresses of machines on the network, the operating systems they use, and the services that they offer. With this information, attacks can be more focused and are less likely to cause alarm. The process of gathering this information is known as network mapping. A ping sweep can be used to determine the IP addresses of the operational hosts on the network by simply observing which addresses respond to a ping message. Port scanning refers to the technique of sequentially contacting (either via a TCP connection request, or via a simple UDP datagram) port numbers on a machine and seeing what happens in response. These responses, in turn, can be used to determine the services offered (for example, HTTP or FTP) by the machine. Attackers also use traceroute to attempt to map the target network. The primary defenses against network mapping are firewalls and intrusion detection systems.

- **Denial of service attacks:** Typically, a DoS attack works by creating so much work for the infrastructure under attack that legitimate work cannot be performed. In a SYN flood attack, the attacker deluges a server with TCP SYN packets, each having a spoofed IP source address. The server, not being able to differentiate between a legitimate SYN and a spoofed SYN, completes the second step of the TCP handshake for a spoofed SYN, allocating data structures and state. The third step of the three-way handshake is never completed by the attacker, leaving an ever-increasing number of partially open connections, and eventually bringing the system to its knees.

- **Distributed denial of service attack (DDoS):** The attacker first gains access to numerous hosts across the Internet (for example, via self-propagating worms) and inserts slave programs in these hosts. Once a large number of such slave programs are running, a master program contacts and instructs each of them to launch a DoS attack directed at the same target host. The resulting coordinated attack is particularly devastating, since it is coming from many directions at once. The primary defenses are over-provisioned bandwidth and upstream rate limiting.

♦ **Defending against attacks: packet filtering.** Packet filters, typically located at gateways to institutional networks, operate by first parsing datagram headers and then applying filtering rules from an administrator-specified rule set to determine whether to drop the datagram. Filtering decisions are typically based on (i) IP source or destination address; (ii) TCP or UDP source and destination port; (iii) ICMP message type; and (iv) connection-initialization datagrams using the TCP SYN or ACK bits. Packet filters can defend against network mapping and DDoS attacks.

♦ **Defending against attacks: cryptography.** There are two classes of cryptography algorithms: symmetric-key cryptography and public-key cryptography. With a symmetric cipher, a message and a key are supplied as input to an encryption algorithm, producing ciphertext. The receiver inputs the ciphertext and key into a decryption algorithm to recover the original plaintext. Importantly, the algorithm is not secret and is known to all. However, the key is known only to the communicating entities. Among the symmetric key algorithms, the textbook focuses on so-called "block ciphers," for which DES and 3DES are examples. In a block cipher, the message is chopped into blocks (for example, 64 bits) and each block is separately encrypted. Thus, (ignoring cipher block chaining), the sender inputs a block and the key into the encryption algorithm to generate an encrypted block. The receiver inputs the encrypted block and the same key into a decryption algorithm to decrypt the block.

♦ **Distributing keys over a network: public-key cryptography.** In a networking environment, with communicating entities often residing in different continents, it is a non-trivial task to distribute the symmetric shared key among the communicating entities. Public-key cryptography can be used for this task. In public-key cryptography, each communicating entity independently generates two keys: a private key and a public key. Each entity makes its public-key available publicly (for example, on a Web page), but keeps its private key private, not showing it to any other entity. Bob and Alice can obtain the same shared key for symmetric-key cryptography as follows: Alice first creates a random key, which will be the shared symmetric key. She now needs to send this key to Bob over the network in such a way that no one else can see it. To this end, she encrypts the symmetric key with Bob's public key, and sends the encrypted message to Bob. To decrypt the message and extract the symmetric key, one needs to apply to the message Bob's private key, which only Bob has. Bob decrypts the key, so that Alice and Bob finally share the same symmetric key. Distributing a symmetric key among communicating entities is a common application of public-key cryptography. There are many applications of public-key cryptography, some of which are discussed in the textbook.

♦ **End-point authentication.** Suppose you want to communicate with Bob, whose IP address you know. You send a message to Bob and Bob responds to you. But how do you know for sure that you are really communicating with Bob? Examining the source IP address is not sufficient, since Trudy can easily spoof Bob's IP address. Protocols for end-system authentication, using nonces and cryptography, are outlined in the textbook.

♦ **Message integrity.** When Bob receives a message from Alice, how does he know that the message hasn't been tampered with, that it is indeed the same message that Alice originally sent? A popular solution to this problem is for Alice to append a message digest to the message. For example, Alice may create the SHA-1 hash of the original message, encrypt it with her private key, and then append the result to the original message. Bob can decrypt the message digest with Alice's public key, and then compare the result with the hash of the received message. If the two are the same, Bob knows that the message he received is indeed the message that Alice sent.

♦ **Secure e-mail: PGP.** PGP is an example of securing an application-layer protocol. The sender applies symmetric-key cryptography to encrypt the message, public-key cryptography to distribute the secret key to the receiver, and a hash function for message integrity.

♦ **Securing a TCP connection: SSL.** Secure sockets layer (SSL) is software that sits between the application layer and TCP on both the client and server sides. Roughly speaking, when one side of the application writes data to the SSL-enhanced TCP connection, SLL encrypts the data and passes it to TCP; SSL at the other side receives data from TCP, decrypts the data, and passes the decrypted data to the other side of the application. Thus, SSL secures a TCP connection. More specifically, for data transfer, SSL creates SSL records, which include the encrypted data along with a message digest for integrity. The SSL records are sent over TCP. Before data transfer, but after the TCP connection is established, there is an SSL handshake, during which the two sides authenticate each other, agree on the cipher schemes to be employed during the SSL session, and establish session keys.

♦ **Secure network layer: IPsec.** IPsec is a suite of protocols that provide security at the network layer. When a chunk of data is sent between two IPsec-enabled hosts, the data is encrypted and a message digest is appended to the data (ensuring data integrity). No matter what the data is—a TCP segment, a UDP segment, or an ICMP message—the data enjoys the blanket coverage provided by IPsec.

♦ **Securing wireless links: WEP and WPA.** The IEEE 802.11 WEP protocol provides authentication and data encryption between a host and a wireless access point (that is, base station) using a symmetric shared key approach. WEP does not specify a key management algorithm, so it is assumed that the host and wireless access point have somehow agreed on the key via an out-of-band method. Authentication is carried out as in the ap4.0 protocol that we developed in Section 8.3. Encryption is done with the RC4 stream cipher, with a different Initialization Vector (IV) used for each frame. WEP, although extensively used, has serious security flaws. A more recent protocol, WPA, is similar in many ways to WEP but is much more secure.

Review Questions

This section provides additional study questions. Answers to each question are provided in the next section.

1. **IPsec.** True or False? Consider sending a stream of packets from Host A to Host B using IPsec. Typically, a new SA will be established for each packet sent in the stream.

2. **IPsec.** True or False? Suppose that TCP is being run over IPsec. If TCP retransmits the same segment, then the encapsulating IP datagrams will have the same sequence number in the IPsec headers.

3. **SSL.** True or False? Suppose Alice and Bob are communicating over an SSL session. Suppose an attacker, who does not have any of the shared keys, inserts a bogus TCP segment into a packet stream with correct TCP checksum and sequence numbers (and correct IP addresses and port numbers). SSL at the receiving side will accept the bogus packet and pass the payload to the receiving application.

4. **Network mapping.** True or False? Suppose you are doing a traceroute from host A to host B, and all routers along the path are configured to never send ICMP messages. Then it is impossible to determine from traceroute the number of routers in the path between A and B.

5. **Port scanning.** True or False? When an attacker does a port scan to determine the open TCP ports on a target host, all of the packets that the attacker sends can have a spoofed IP address.

6. **TCP hijacking.** Suppose Alice and Bob are interacting via a TCP session, and that Trudy is on a broadcast segment where traffic passes between Alice and Bob.

   a. In 40 words or less, describe how Trudy can masquerade as Alice and hijack the session.

   b. In 40 words or less, why will Bob quickly drop the TCP session with the basic approach?

7. **Public-key cryptography.** Consider RSA with $p = 17$ and $q = 11$.

   a. What are n and z?

   b. Let e be 7. Why is this an acceptable choice for e?

   c. Find d such that $de = 1 \pmod{160}$ and $d < 160$.

   d. Encrypt the message m with $m = 88$ using the key (n, e). Let c denote the corresponding ciphertext. Show all work. Hint: To simplify the calculations, use the following fact:

   $$[(a \bmod n) \times (b \bmod n)] \bmod n = (a \times b) \bmod n$$

   e. Decrypt c. Show all work. Again use the above fact.

8.   **SSL.** Consider the Ethereal screenshot shown below for a portion of an SSL session.

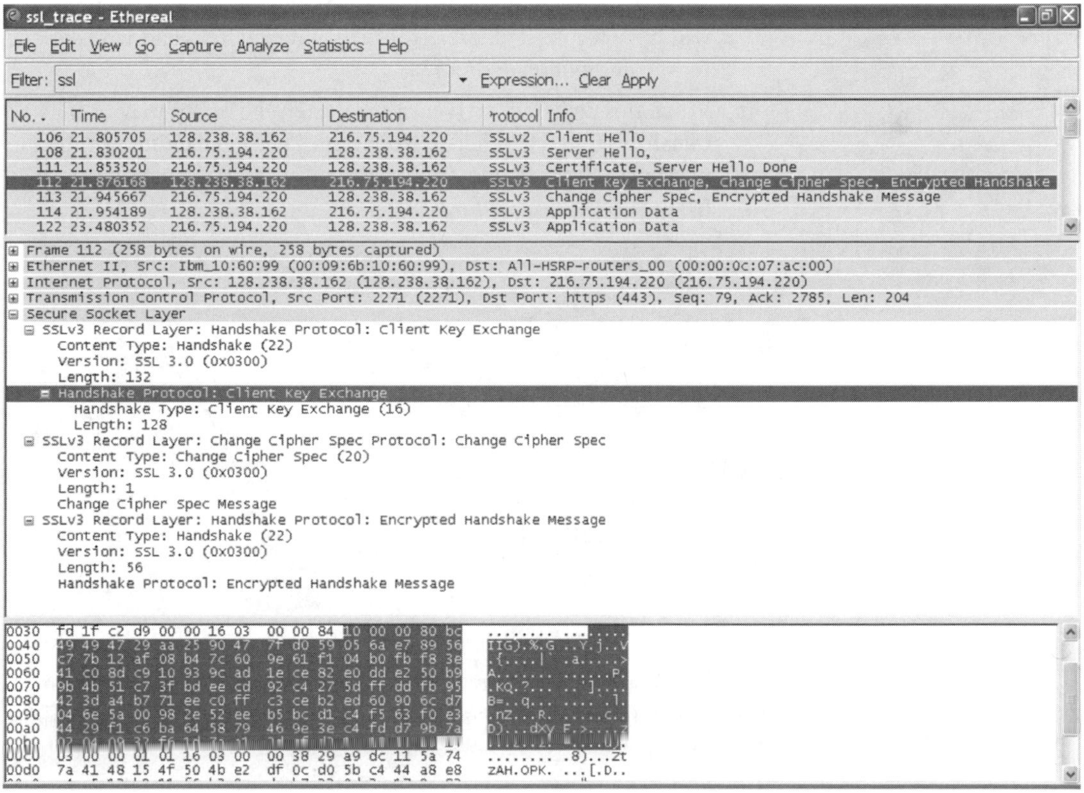

a. Is Ethernet packet 112 sent by the client or server?

b. What is server's IP address and port number?

c. Assuming no loss and no retransmissions, what will be the sequence number of the next TCP segment sent by the client?

d. How many SSL records does Ethernet packet 112 contain?

e. Does packet 112 contain a master secret or an encrypted master secret or neither?

f. Assuming that the handshake type field is one byte and each length field is three bytes, what are the values of the first and last bytes of the master secret (or encrypted master secret)?

g. The client encrypted handshake message takes into account how many SSL records?

h. The server encrypted handshake message takes into account how many SSL records?

9. **IPsec.** Consider the network below. Suppose that the remote host and server communicate with the ESP protocol in tunnel mode.

    a. An IP datagram emitted by the server and destined to the remote host will have whose IP address for the source address and whose IP address for the destination address?

    b. When this datagram arrives at the router, the router may or may not transform it into another IP datagram. The IP datagram sent by the router will have whose IP address for the source address and whose IP address for the destination address?

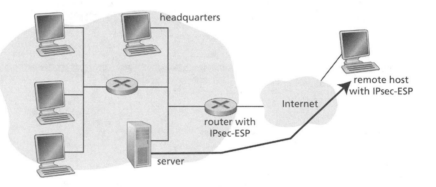

10. **PGP.** Suppose Alice sends a message m to Bob using PGP with integrity and confidentiality. Using (some or all of) the notation m, K_S, $K_S( )$, $K_B^+( )$, $K_B^-( )$, $K_A^+( )$, $K_A^-( )$, $H( )$, $H(m)$, describe what Bob does to authenticate and decrypt the message.

Answers to Review Questions

1. False. After establishing SAs to each other, all the packets sent between the hosts will use these SAs with the same session keys.

2. False. IPsec at the source increments the sequence number every time the source sends a new datagram. Since the two (identical) segments will be sent within different diagrams, the two datagrams will have different sequence numbers.

3. False. SSL sends records, each of which includes a message digest. To create the message digest, one needs a shared key, which the attacker doesn't have.

4. False. With traceroute, the source host sends a series of packets, incrementing the TTL for each packet. Eventually one of the packets reaches the destination host; when it does, the destination message sends back an error message. The source host can determine the number of intermediate routers from the TTL of the packet that reached the destination host.

5. False. To determine if a TCP port is open, the attacker sends a TCP SYN segment and waits for a response (a TCP SYN/ACK segment if the port is open). If the source IP address is spoofed in the TCP SYN segment, then the response will go to the spoofed address rather than to the attacker's IP address. Thus the attacker will never know if a SYN/ACK was sent or not, and thus will not learn if the port is open.

6. a. Trudy can sniff the packets sent between Alice and Bob and determine the IP addresses and port numbers they are using. Trudy can also sniff the sequence numbers in Alice's packets and determine the sequence number for Alice's next packet. Trudy can then masquerade as Alice by sending Bob segments with the correct port numbers, sequence numbers, and acknowledgement numbers.

   b. Bob will acknowledge Trudy's packets; Alice will see the acknowledgements for data that she never sent; Alice will send new acknowledgements, corresponding to the bytes she actually sent; Bob will receive two sets of inconsistent acknowledgments (from Alice and Trudy) and drop the connection.

7. a. $n = pq = 187; z = (p - 1)(q - 1) = 160$

   b. $e = 7$ is acceptable since it is relative prime with $z = 160$.

   c. $d = 23$

   d. $c = m^e \bmod n = 88^7 \bmod 187 = 11$

   e. $m = c^d \bmod n = 11^{23} \bmod 187 = 88$

8.   a.   Sent by client.

      b.   The server's IP address is 216.75.194.220 and port number is 443.

      c.   The sequence number of the next TCP segment sent by the client will be $79 + 204 = 283$.

      d.   Ethernet packet 112 contains 3 SSL records.

      e.   Packet 112 contains the encrypted secret.

      f.   First byte: BC; last byte: 29

      g.   The client encrypted handshake message takes into account 6 SSL records.

      h.   The server encrypted handshake message takes into account 8 SSL records.

9.   a.   Source address = server's IP address; destination address = remote host's IP address.

      b.   Source address = router interface IP address; destination address = remote host's IP address.

10.   Bob first extracts $K_B^+(K_S)$ and $K_S(m + K_A^-(H(m)))$ from the "package" he receives from Alice. He then applies $K_B^-(\ )$ to $K_B^+(K_S)$ to obtain the session key K_S. He then applies K_S to $K_S(m + K_A^-(H(m)))$ to obtain both m and $K_A^-(H(m))$. He now has the unencrypted message, but it remains to verify the message's integrity. To this end, he applies $K_A^+(\ )$ to $K_A^-(H(m))$ to obtain $x = H(m)$. He then applies $H(\ )$ to the received message m. If the result is x, he concludes that the message is authentic.

9

Network Management

Most Important Ideas and Concepts from Chapter 9

Although Chapter 9 is the shortest chapter in our textbook, network management is an important topic nonetheless with important ideas and concepts that one should take away from this chapter. We discuss only five important ideas below (rather than our usual ten), not only to reflect the chapter's short length, but also to assure you that the concepts below are indeed important. Rather than forcing ourselves to choose an arbitrary number of topics (ten), we list and discuss the network management topics that we believe are truly important and most deserving to be singled out for emphasis.

♦ **Network management framework: managed device (managed objects, management information base, management agent), managing entity, and network management protocol.** Figure 9.2 on page 735 of the textbook illustrates the conceptual framework for network management. First and foremost, there are *managed devices*—the network equipment, both hardware and software, that make up the network. Each managed device may have many components, or managed objects. A managed object may be a physical part of the device (for example, an interface card) or a piece of software (for example, a protocol such as RIP or TCP). Information about a managed object is contained in a *management information base (MIB)* in the managed device. A MIB might contain the number of checksum errors encountered in frames on an Ethernet interface, or the number of UDP segments received by a host. The *management agent* is a software process associated with a device that communicates with the network's *managing entity*. The managing entity is also a software process. It receives information from the managed devices and, together with humans-in-the-loop, issues commands that control the managed devices. The protocol used for communication between the managing entity and each managed device is the *network management protocol*. Often, the term "network management protocol" is considered synonymous with "network management." However, now that we've studied Chapter 9, we know that the network management protocol is only a part (albeit a very important part) of the larger network management framework.

♦ **SNMP protocol.** The SNMP protocol is the Internet Standard protocol (RFC 3416) for communication between managed devices and the managing entity. SNMP can be used in two different ways: In *request-response mode*, the managing entity sends an SNMP request message to the agent in the managed device. This SNMP request is typically used to query or set (for example, initialize) a MIB object value in the managed device. The agent in the managed device then replies to the SNMP request message with an SNMP response message. In *trap-mode*, a managed device sends an SNMP trap message to the managing entity on its own initiative, that is, without having first received a request message from the managing entity. A trap message typically informs the managing entity that an exceptional condition has occurred (for example, an interface has gone down). In this sense, a trap message is much like a hardware or software interrupt in a computer—it informs the controlling entity (the operating system in the case of the computer or the managing entity in the case of a managed network) that a noteworthy event has occurred. On receiving the interrupt/SNMP trap, the computer/managing entity can then take appropriate actions in response to the interrupt/trap.

♦ **The need for presentation services.** If all computers represented and stored information exactly the same way, there would be no need for a presentation service. But alas, in spite of standards, different computers have different ways of representing and storing information internally. Perhaps the most well-known example of such a difference is the fact that some computers store the bytes that make up an integer value in most-significant-byte-first order; other computers store the bytes that make up an integer in exactly the opposite order—in least-significant-byte-first order!

But what does byte ordering in computers have to do with communication? Recall that when a communication protocol sends data from one computer to another, it is simply sending a stream of bytes. Thus, if a sender transmits the bytes representing an integer that is stored most-significant-byte-first at the sender to a receiver that interprets/stores an integer least-significant-byte-first, then the integer value sent by the sender will be interpreted as a very *different* integer value by the receiver. The role of presentation services is to solve such problems, ensuring that the *meaning* of the information communicated (for example, the numerical value of an integer) rather than the underlying representation of the information (for example, most-significant-byte-first, or least-significant-byte-first order) is preserved. Figures 9.7 and 9.8 on page 755 of the textbook provide a more whimsical illustration of the presentation problem, using the analogy of an aging hippie, a grandmother, and a teenager, each of whom has a very different way of internally representing the idea that something is pleasing.

♦ **Type, Length, Value (TLV) encoding.** Suppose that two computers want to exchange a piece of information, while preserving the meaning of this information (for example, in our example above, the value of an integer rather than the verbatim internal representation of this integer). A natural way for them to do this is to agree on a predefined data format. The so-called Type, Length, Value (TLV) encoding is one way to achieve this. The TLV encoding of a piece of data indicates the *type* (*T*) of the data (which must be one of a set of predefined data types); the number of bytes needed to express the value of the data (that is, the *length* (*L*) of the data), and the *value* (*V*) of the data itself (in some predetermined format, agreed to by all). TLV encoding is sometimes referred to as *self-identifying encoding*, since every TLV-encoded piece of data explicitly carries its data type (that is, is self-identifying) as part of its encoding.

♦ **Abstract Syntax Notation One (ASN.1).** ASN.1 is an ISO standard for data representation. ASN.1 has a set of predefined data types (for example, Boolean, integer, real, character string, object name) and a set of rules that define the TVL encoding for these data types. Data to be transmitted in ASN.1 format is encoded using ASN.1's TLV encoding rules (known as Basic Encoding Rules, in ASN.1 parlance) before being sent from sender to receiver. The receiver, knowing that the data it is receiving is ASN.1-encoded (because the protocol *requires* all data to be encoded using ASN.1), can use the ASN.1 syntax to decode the data, and then locally store the data according to its own local data format/storage conventions.

Review Questions

This section provides additional study questions. Answers to each question are provided in the next section.

1. **Request-Response versus trap mode.** Suppose that a network operator wants to be notified immediately if a link interface goes down. Should this notification be performed using SNMP in request-response mode, or in trap-mode? Why?

2. **TLV or TVL coding?** Why do you think the length precedes the value in a TLV encoding (rather than the length following the value)?

3. **ASN.1.** What is the ASN.1 object identifier for the TCP protocol? (See Figure 9.3 on page 744 of the textbook.)

4. **ASN.1 (more).** What is the ASN.1 object identifier for the MIB variable that counts "the total number of [TCP] segments received, including those received in error. This count includes segments received on currently established connections." [RFC 1213]? (To answer this question, refer to RFC 1213, or better yet, use the online interactive ASN.1 object identifier tree at http://www.alvestrand.no/objectid.)

5. **SNMP.** Suppose that the network managing entity wants to send an SNMP message to a host to query that host for the "the total number of [TCP] segments received, including those received in error. This count includes segments received on currently established connections." [RFC 1213]. Consider Figure 9.4 on page 748 of the textbook. What are the values in the fields of the SNMP message sent to the host? (In order to answer this question, you will need to do some background investigation. Consult RFC 3416, page 6 to determine the type value for the SNMP GET request. To get the size and range of possible request ID values, and the values for the Error Status and Error Index field, see RFC 3416, page 7. The name field of the SNMP MIB variable being queried contains the ASN.1 object identifier tree value of that SNMP MIB variable; therefore, see the answer to Review Question 4.)

6. **ASN.1 BER.** Consider Figure 9.9 on page 757 of the textbook. What is the ASN.1 BER encoding of {weight, 129} {lastname, "Chopin"}?

7. **ASN.1 BER (more).** Consider Figure 9.9 again. What is the ASN.1 BER encoding of {weight, 262} {lastname, "Beethoven"}?

Answers to Review Questions

1. Trap mode. In request-response mode, the operator would have to probe the device continuously, checking that the interface is up. If the operator sends a probe every T time units, then on average, the operator would find out that a link has gone down T/2 time units after the event has occurred. Also, if the link is normally up, there is a high overhead to this polling—most SNMP request and response messages would be sent simply to determine that the link is (still) up. In trap mode, a single SNMP message will be generated as soon as the link goes down.

2. The length precedes the value so that after determining the length, the receiver knows exactly how many of the subsequent bytes constitute the value. Recall that some data types (for example, character strings) can be of arbitrary length; therefore, the receiver needs to know where in the ensuing stream of bytes the value ends.

3. 1.3.6.1.2.1.6

4. 1.3.6.1.2.1.6.10. See http://www.alvestrand.no/objectid/1.3.6.1.2.1.6.html

5.

PDU type: 0   /* the GET request has type 0)

Request Id: <an integer value put here by the managing entity>

                   /* per RFC 3416, range is (-214783648..214783647) */

Error Status: 0   /* this field not used for a GET */

Error Index: 0   /* this field not used for a GET */

Object identifier 1: 1.3.6.1.2.1.6.10

Value: NULL   /* NULL is an ASN.1-defined data type */

6. 4 6 C h o p i n 2 1 '10000001'.

   The 4 indicates that the first data item is an octet string (see Table 9.5 on page 756 of the textbook). The 6 indicates that there are six letters following. This is the ASN.1 BER encoding of the character string "Chopin". The 2 indicates that the next item is an integer. The 1 indicates that the integer value is one byte long. The binary value '1000001' is the binary representation of the number 129.

7. 4 9 B e e t h o v e n 2 2 '00000001' '00000110'.

   The last two bytes are the binary representation of the number 262.